Here's what these famous men might have said about

# The Young Man's Guide to
# Awesomeness.

(If they weren't already dead.)

"I won the Congressional Medal of Honor and the Nobel Prize. I founded the National Park system. I climbed the Matterhorn on my honeymoon and volunteered to fight in WWI after serving as the youngest president. I wanted to write a book called "The Young Man's Guide to Awesomeness" before I died, but I was too busy being awesome. I'm glad that Barrett Johnson did. My book would have been better, but this one is pretty good, too."

Teddy Roosevelt,
26th President and All-Around Manly Man

"Nothing impresses the ladies like killing a giant nocturnal rodent, peeling off it's skin and wearing it on your head. They really dig that. Girls also like guys who do what this book says. Trust me: if you read this book AND wear a coonskin hat, you'll be absolutely irresistible."

Davy Crockett,
Famed Hunter, Trapper, Congressman, and Alamo Hero

"On May 14, 1804, I invited my friend Meriwether Lewis to go camping overnight in the woods outside of St. Louis, Missouri. What I didn't tell him is that the President had tasked us to explore the West. For the next two and a half years, I convinced Lewis that we were lost and couldn't remember where our campsite was. He had no idea that he was actually part of one of the greatest pranks of all time. It just shows that life's big, important adventures can also be a blast. This book shows that, too."

William Clark,
World Famous Explorer


"The sacrificial courage you saw me display in the movie *Hacksaw Ridge* is stuff I learned following Jesus. It's also quite rare in today's culture. This book will show you how an ordinary guy like you can have an extraordinary life -- maybe even land a movie deal."

Desmond Doss
Army Medic and American Hero

# The Young Man's Guide to
# AWESOMENESS

## How to Guard Your Heart
## Get the Girl
## and Save the World

Barrett Johnson

INFO FOR
FAMILIES
resources

# The Young Man's Guide to Awesomeness
## How to Guard your Heart, Get the Girl and Save the World

© 2017 by Barrett Johnson

An INFO for Families Resource
www.INFOforFamilies.com

Printed in the United States of America

Art Design by Emilie Johnson

ISBN 13: 978-1541160095

# For Christian, Landon, and Drew.

"You guys have what it takes to be awesome."

# Inside This Guide:

# Introduction

*Read this first. Seriously. It's important.*

If you're reading these words, I'm going to assume a few things:

First off, I'm going to assume that you're a guy. You're probably in your teens. You're the target audience for this book, so that makes sense. If you are a woman (or a man over 25), you need to move along. There's nothing to see here.

Secondly, I'm going to assume that you want to have a life that means something. After all, that's what this book is about. If you weren't at least a little bit curious, you wouldn't be here.

Third, I realize that a parent or another adult probably gave you this book. That's okay. They know stuff that you don't know and they think this book will help you out. It shows they care about you. You should give them a hug or something.

Finally, I'm going to assume that you don't like to read. How can I assume that? Because you're a guy. And most guys don't like to read. That's why this book is relatively short. I also included links to some short videos that you can watch as you read. I did that for you and your YouTube-watching, video-game playing, chronically-short attention-spanned self. You're welcome.

So, if you fit the profile, let's cut to the chase and deal with the question that I'm sure you're asking in your head right now: "Is this a book about sex?"

The answer is yes. And no.

Yes, we're going to talk about the fact that you are a sexual being. And how the sex drive *that God gave you* is a very good thing. But we're also going to talk honestly about how your sex drive has the power to derail your life. In big ways. It happens all the time to guys just like you and I want to help you avoid that.

But no, this book isn't just about sex. You'll discover what it looks like to be a young man whose life means something. You'll realize how critically important your thought life is. You'll see how walking with God and using your strength for His purposes can make your life amazing. And if you have noticed that girls are pretty cool, you'll learn about how being the right kind of guy will attract the right kind of girl. So when it comes down to it, maybe this book is all about sex after all.

---

Know that this is NOT a "sex is bad" book.

Actually, it's a "sex is awesome" book.

---

God created sex and He wants you to experience it in the right time and in the right way. (Box: Hint: that means within the safe boundaries of a heterosexual marriage relationship.) Unfortunately, because of the hyper-sexualized culture in which you live, young men today have a very high chance of messing up their sexuality. The stuff in this book is designed to help you not to do that.

2

All the research out there says that guys like you are struggling. The porn epidemic (which we will get to early on) is messing with the hearts and minds of an entire generation. Do you want to know what else the research tells us? It tells us that young men desperately want help to deal with it. If that's you, then keep reading.

In a broader sense, this book is designed to help you to build a life that matters; to be awesome.

## What To Look For As You Read

I have tried hard to make this thing really easy for you to read. In every chapter of this "guide to awesomeness," you're going to find six key elements. I wanted to tell you about them up front so you can be on the lookout for them.

 **1. The Big Idea**: This is a principle that is foundational for your life. It is important stuff so be sure to pay close attention.

**2. Listen to Your Body**: Different parts of your body will serve as reminders of the truths you discover.

 **3. How Most Guys Operate**: You'll see the typical thinking of the average teenage guy today. This is w h e r e most guys out there are getting it wrong. (Don't forget that most guys are morons.)

**4. How You Can Be Different**: In contrast to all the morons out there, you'll see how God offers a better way to think, act and live. It won't be easy, but you can do it. And your life will be truly extraordinary.

## 5. From the Life of David: This will be

something you can learn from an awesome (but flawed) man in the Bible. Sometimes we will look at someone close to him.

 **6. Take Action**: These are key things you should start doing right now. Some guys might read this entire book and never do anything about it. That would be a waste. So act on what you read.

What you're going to read in this book is a bit unconventional. Not a lot of people are talking about sexual purity and chivalry and living a life of purpose while you're still in your teens. But everything you'll read here is true. If you take time to watch the videos we collected for this book, you'll hear some stories of real life guys who have experienced it first-hand.

# One Final Suggestion:

There's something you can do that will help make this book even more meaningful: read it with someone who is older than you and talk about it as you go. You might discover that this stuff is perfect to process with a parent or another key adult in your life.

He has seen and done things that you don't know about yet. So his insight might be very helpful to you. I have even included some discussion questions at the end of every chapter that might give you some things to talk about.

So let's get moving. Time is short and your life is happening already. Read on...

-Barrett Johnson

P.S. I'd love to meet you. You can find a video clip titled "Introduction" (and all the other videos I told you about) at www.infoforfamilies.com/awesome. I will be sending you there a lot, so you might want to bookmark that page on your computer or device.

P.S.S. If you have a smartphone and want to access the videos really easily, I have included a QR code for each one. (If you don't know what that is, search your app store for "QR Reader." Then you simply scan the code in the book and the clip will immediately pop up on your phone. ) It's really cool.

## Here's the code for the first video. Give it a try before moving on.

# 1. Moving Towards Awesomeness

*"God is saying. . .Write a good story, take somebody with you and let Me help." – Donald Miller*

Watch "Chapter 1 - Moving Towards Awesomeness"
at www.infoforfamilies.com/awesome.)

Everybody loves a great story. Whether it's a blockbuster movie or a novel you can't put down, powerful stories have a way of holding your attention. They put you on the edge of your seat, constantly leaving you wondering what will happen next.

An awesome story will typically have a few key elements. It will have a lead character you are pulling for. He may be flawed, but he's a guy you care about. He usually has a clear goal that he's trying to achieve. As he pursues his goal, there are some challenges he must overcome. And there will almost certainly be a girl involved. There's always a girl.

Think about the movies guys like. Every blockbuster movie from Star Wars to Spiderman contains these elements. They are critical to telling a great story.

Here's what most guys don't realize: what works in a story also works in your life.

If you want to have an awesome life, then you need to see your life like you see a powerful movie. You need the same foundational elements that a movie has. You need to be the type of person that others can pull for. You need to want something big with your life. You need to courageously face the challenges you encounter. And along the way, it would be great if you found the perfect girl.

> Nobody stumbles into an awesome life. It doesn't just happen because you get lucky. No, an awesome life happens when you build your life on the right things and do things in the right way.

Sure, there are a few exceptions to this truth. Somebody is going to win the lottery. A few exceptional people will see their YouTube channel go viral, but the odds are never in your favor of that happening. Plus, there's no promise that being rich or famous will result in a satisfying life. When you dig deeper, most rich and famous people will tell you that their money and fame has made them miserable. Some of the happiest people live very simple lives.

# Three Big Things

God has placed some fundamental things in the soul of every man that help him to tell a great story. From the early days of adolescence until the day you die, these things will be present in your life. They include the private thoughts that drive your actions, your desire to connect with a woman, and your longing for a life of adventure.

These three things are at the foundation of a life of awesomeness. Get them right and you'll be on your way to building a life that means something. Get them wrong and you'll miss out on God's very best for you. That's why we have organized this book into three sections: how to guard your heart, get the girl, and save the world.

# 1. How to Guard Your Heart

A few pages ago, you read that this is (sort of) a book about sex. That's because God has made you a sexual being with the amazing potential to connect with a woman in a very unique way. (We could draw pictures but that would be weird.) While you are so much more than just a sexual being, the truth is that your sexuality has the real potential to blow up your life.

Most sexual sins begin in the private thoughts of your heart and mind. Even if you never act on them, they are still sinful. They still have an effect on your life. In many ways, your thoughts have the power to dictate the person you become. More on that in the next chapter.

Before we get any further on this subject, we need to be clear about something: God is pro-sex. He invented it. He wants you to have a great sex life. But be sure of this: whatever God makes the most awesome and beautiful and satisfying for the people He created, are the very things that God's enemy will try to screw up for us. This is DEFINITELY true about sex.

What should be the source of some of our greatest joy is, in many people's lives, the source of their greatest pain. It's hard to build an awesome life when you're carrying around a bunch of shame and guilt from sexual sin. That's why it's worth talking about here. That's why we're going to speak very specifically about your thought life and pornography and some other ways that your private life can get you into trouble.

## 2. How to Get The Girl

There's this strange transition that every teenage guy goes through in how he sees the opposite sex. Before it occurs, girls are weird, gross, and a waste of time. Then something changes. Suddenly, girls are interesting. They smell nice. Their curves and their looks are all you can think about. If you haven't yet experienced this shift, just wait. It will happen soon enough.

As you grow into manhood, you're probably going to want to connect with a girl. Again, this is something that God has put into the heart of most every man. Sadly, many guys rush into it before they are ready. Also, because they operate from a place of selfishness, they often do it the wrong way. This can lead to some complications. More on that later.

What you need to know now is that the way you interact with girls now will impact how you connect with a wife for the vast majority of your life. While adulthood and marriage may seem like they are a million miles away, they will get here sooner than you think. And what you do now matters. You might think that is nuts, but ask any married man and he will tell you that it's true.

## 3. How to Save The World

If God has put a desire for adventure into every man (and He has), then you have the obligation to build a thrilling life. Sadly, too many guys channel all their energy into fake adventures.

They immerse themselves in video games or movies in an attempt to experience something exciting. While this form of escapism can be fun for a while, it's no substitute for a truly interesting life.

You may be thinking that life is boring. Let me assure you, life is not boring. Granted, it could be that *your* life is boring simply because you are telling a boring story. You are settling for a counterfeit adventure. That's on you, and you have the power to change that.

> "The internet is so big, so powerful and pointless that for some people it is a complete substitute for life." –Andrew Brown

The final section of this "guide to awesomeness" focuses on how you can save the world. While that may sound like an unrealistic goal, I assure you that it is not. You have the real opportunity to choose a life that enables you to join God in His story of saving the world. You can do things that will echo in eternity. You can build a life that matters and be a person that God can use for big things.

## It's a Different World

The stuff we will address in this book is for young men today. Some of it wouldn't be relevant 10 years ago because our world has changed so dramatically.

Thanks to the technology that most teenagers carry in their pockets, an endless supply of entertainment is always close. This includes highly-sexualized content that is easy to access. This has significantly changed the way young people come to experience their sexuality. It affects how you see girls, how you enter relationships, and even how your brain works.

It's like an entire generation has been part of a decade-long experiment on how this stuff will impact your lives -- and the results are just now coming in. You need to know that the findings are not good. The world (who doesn't care about you) thought that removing any boundaries about your sexuality would be a good thing. They were very, very wrong.

Much of what you're going to read here is an attempt to offer a better approach to managing your life, including the part of you that wants to connect with a girl. It is rooted in God's design for sex and relationships. In contrast to the world, God cares about you more than you know. He knows what is best and He offers this to you. That leads us to the first "big idea" that you need to know.

# THE BIG IDEA:

### Following God's plan is the foundation of a great life.

Our culture's idea of what is true and good is constantly changing. Year by year, the world's technology gets better, its values get worse, and its people become more confused. Our freedoms have convinced us that we have the power to define what is right and wrong in our own eyes. While God certainly gives us this liberty, we reject His truth at our own risk.

At its core, the Bible is essentially God telling you this: *"Young man, this is the way I made the world to work. The laws, directives, and guidelines I am giving you are for your good. If you do the things I tell you and align your life with these truths, things will go well for you. If you ignore them, your life will always be frustrating and unsatisfying."*

So from the start, I encourage you to seriously consider how you see God's Word. Do you believe it's true? Do you believe it has what you need to build an awesome life? Do you trust God enough to look to Him for direction?

## LISTEN TO YOUR BODY:
# "I am your manhood."

Your penis. (Yes, this just got awkward.) This body part is what makes you a man. God said that your being a man is "very good," so this part of you is very good. Unfortunately, this single part of your body has the real potential to get you into very big trouble. This has played out historically as millions of well-intentioned guys have imploded their lives because they couldn't control their sex drives.

Because it would be weird to spend an entire book talking about your junk, we're going to try something different. In each of the chapters that follow, we're going to talk about a bunch of other body parts. Ones that are not near as – um – personal.

Hopefully, you'll see that managing the rest of your parts will help keep your manhood from getting you into significant trouble.

## HOW MOST GUYS OPERATE

Most people in our world can be consistently expected to do one thing: what everyone else is doing. They join the masses in embracing what everyone else says is cool, fashionable, and popular. While individuals might insist that they are non-conformists and that they do what they want, their behavior shows that they usually blend in with everyone else rather effectively.

When it comes to the typical teenage guy and how he manages his heart, interacts with girls, and plans for the future, he will usually do what everyone else is doing. He doesn't give much thought to how he thinks. He sees girls as something to pursue. He sees the future as very far away, so he lives mainly for today.

The reality is that most guys are not intentional with their lives. They aren't aiming for any target, and they don't have any plan to get there. Most importantly, most guys today are missing a clear standard of character and belief that guides their decisions. They just do whatever feels right in the moment.

## HOW YOU CAN BE DIFFERENT

You want something better. You are willing to consider what it takes to create something awesome with your life. In addition, you realize how easily you can derail your life with sexual sin, so you are committed to taking steps to prevent that.

In Psalm 119:9, the author (probably David) asks the question that we all want to know the answer to: *"How can a young man stay on the path of purity?"* He immediately answers the question for teenage guys everywhere: *"By living according to your word."*

You're going to see a lot of Scripture in the pages to come, so give careful consideration to what you read and how it applies to your life. A young man who strives to follow these truths will set himself apart from every other guy out there. It is the foundation of building a life of awesomeness.

# FROM THE LIFE OF DAVID

One of the first Bible characters that kids learn about in Sunday School is David. From the moment he was chosen to be king while still a teenager, David lived a pretty awesome life. He was a warrior, a poet, and a popular leader who was loved by his people. He was also a regular guy who struggled with the exact same things that you struggle with.

Even though we know him as a hero, he did some pretty foolish things in his day. One boneheaded thing in particular was that he had multiple wives. (At the same time.) Being a husband to one woman is hard enough. Being a husband to seven or eight is just idiotic.

In addition, David committed some spectacular sins along the way. This got him into spectacular trouble. But you will see that he did something about his disobedience. He responded to his sin in the right way.

After all he experienced and lived through (which you will read about in the coming chapters), David offers some advice in Psalm 19:7-11. Read his reflection on what he learned along the way:

*The law of the LORD is perfect, refreshing the soul.*
*The statutes of the LORD are trustworthy, making wise the simple.*
*The precepts of the LORD are right, giving joy to the heart.*
*The commands of the LORD are radiant, giving light to the eyes.*
*The fear of the LORD is pure, enduring forever.*
*The decrees of the LORD are firm, and all of them are righteous.*
*They are more precious than gold, than much pure gold;*
*They are sweeter than honey, than honey from the honeycomb.*
*By them your servant is warned; in keeping them there is great reward.*

David describes the value of trusting in God's Word. He uses words like law, statues, precepts, commands, fear and decrees to describe the Scriptures. He stresses how valuable they are to you. Then he concludes that there is great reward in life when you align your life with God's ways. This is critical to finding the awesome life that God promises you.

When this book holds up a Bible verse for you to consider, don't rush through it. Take a minute to consider that perhaps the God who made you knows exactly what He is talking about. You might want to consider what He says.

# TAKE ACTION

So what are some steps you can take right now as you work through this guide to awesomeness? Here are a few places to start:

## 1. Read with an open mind.

You're going to encounter some things in this book that are a bit counter-cultural. They may not line up with what the majority of people you know are thinking or doing. But as you read, I hope you are open to what God is trying to tell you. It will help if you read with a desire to learn.

## 2. Believe that God's ways are best.

As you consider building your life differently than most of your peers, it will help if you trust God. Believe that He knows what He is talking about. Have confidence that if you focus on the things that God says matters, your life will begin to matter.

## 3. Commit yourself to changing.

You might encounter something here that requires you to significantly adjust your life. You might have to stop a bad habit, start doing something that is brand new to you or deal with some secret sin. Know that God wants to help you change whatever needs changing in your life.

Now that you have a general idea of where we are heading, you are ready to go. You are on your way to being awesome. But you need to know just a few more things:

In the course of your reading, don't forget to pause and watch the supplemental videos. Each of them is pretty short and they will all include something that is worth seeing. If you come to one (usually at the beginning and end of each chapter), just set the book down for a minute and watch the clip before you continue reading. I'm sure you'll appreciate the diversion.

Also, you may want to write in this book, scribbling notes or underlining things that jump out at you. That's okay. It's your book. Do with it what you want.

Finally, don't forget to use the discussion questions to talk about this with someone older than you. It will help make this more meaningful. Trust me on this.

Watch the video called "Chapter 1 – Matt's Story" at www.infoforfamilies.com/awesome.

# TALK ABOUT IT

1. Who do you know that is telling an awesome story with their life? What makes it so interesting? What part do you think God plays in it?

2. Our world has rejected God's truth in favor of letting everybody decide what is right in their own eyes. Do you think that has made things better or worse? Why?

3. What are some examples of men imploding their lives because they couldn't control their sex drive? Think of celebrities, Bible characters, and even people you know.

Army recruiter?
You mean travel agent?

# 2. Taking Control of Your Thought Life

*"Our life is what our thoughts make it." – Marcus Aurelius*

Watch "Chapter 2 – Taking Control of Your Thought Life" at www.infoforfamilies.com/awesome.

A few years ago my family had the chance to visit Carlsbad Caverns in New Mexico, one of the nation's largest cave systems. It was truly breathtaking to explore expansive caves bigger than indoor football stadiums that were nearly a thousand feet underground.

What struck me as most unique were the systems of stalactites and stalagmites. As water slowly drips from the ceiling, it leaves microscopic limestone deposits, creating giant stone icicles hanging from the ceiling. Where the drops hit the ground, tiny limestone nubs grow into towers of solid rock, some as tall as trees; others the size of school buses.

This formation process doesn't happen quickly. In fact, it takes thousands of years for these massive stalagmites to grow. But as they grow, they become more solid and established. Over time, they become a permanent part of the caverns.

This slow but purposeful process of growth is similar to what happens to your heart. Every time your mind gives attention to a thought, it sinks into your soul, just as a drop of water makes a small limestone deposit in a cave. Given enough time and enough repetition, it begins to grow and define your character. You slowly become who you are based upon a million tiny thoughts and decisions you make every day.

This is both good news and bad news, depending on what you are thinking about. You see, your brain is hardwired to repeat thoughts and behaviors that it finds pleasurable. These things trigger a release of dopamine, leaving you craving more and more of whatever it is that your brain (and you) like.

But there is some bad news: your brain is like a computer that doesn't know right from wrong. It will respond by saying "more, please" to anything it likes, even if that thing is destructive. You can enjoy ice cream three meals a day, but that doesn't mean it's a good thing.

Bad habits are created when your brain says, "more, please" to all the wrong things. Alcoholics and sex addicts know this all too well. They know that what they are doing is destroying their lives and relationships, but they just can't stop.

> Most sex addicts testify that they got hooked when they were teenagers.

Studies show that what you think about (especially if the thoughts are of a sexual nature) has the power to define how you feel about yourself and impact how you function in the world. For many guys, small sexual thoughts turn to frequent sexual thoughts, which become habitual thoughts. You eventually find it difficult to think about anything else.

In contrast, good habits are created when you brain is trained to say, "more, please" to things that build your character. People who create awesome learn to filter out thoughts that are unhelpful so they can focus on what matters.

Lives of substance and meaning are built over a long period of time, just like a stalagmite is built. That's why it's so important to understand the power of your thought life. Because what you think about is ultimately what you will become.

# THE BIG IDEA:

## Your mind can be your greatest ally or your greatest enemy.

Most of the great things you will do in life will start with a thought. You will have an idea for something creative or you will picture the type of life you want to have or a girl you want to pursue. Perhaps God will show you something that you need to do for Him. If these things are rooted in your passions and convictions, your mind will focus on these thoughts more than anything else.

Unfortunately, most of the boneheaded things you do in your life will also start with a thought. Your mind will suggest a course of action that you know is wrong. The more you entertain the idea, the more it sounds like a good one. If you let it develop long enough, you can find yourself acting on it, even though you know it's not in your best interest.

How do potential thoughts (both good and bad) get into your mind? You allow them in. The things you watch, read, and listen to all get filed away in your mind.

That's why this entire section is rooted in how you "guard your heart." For our purposes, your heart refers to the deepest part of your soul and mind, the core of your life.

Proverbs 4:23 puts this command so clearly, *"Above all else, guard your heart, for everything you do flows from it."* That verse is both simple and exactly right. Everything you do stems from the condition of your heart and mind.

## LISTEN TO YOUR BODY

# "I AM YOUR BRAIN."

How you manage me, the pink matter tucked inside your skull, will determine the course of your life. Left to wander where it wants to go, your thoughts can go to some pretty dark places. And it WILL if you let it. Because it does what you tell it to do. But, when you intentionally submit your thoughts to God, you are on your way to an awesome life.

# HOW MOST GUYS OPERATE

Let's be completely honest here. Most guys don't think about this issue at all. They are careless with their hearts and minds. They let their thoughts run wild and go wherever they want with no regard as to whether what they are thinking is good or bad. They give no consideration as to whether their thoughts are helpful or destructive.

As with much of their lives, their thought life is pretty undisciplined. To put it simply, they don't think about what they are thinking. They rarely consider their thoughts or try to regulate or control them.

With regards to sexual and/or impure thoughts, they don't see anything wrong with them. They fill their minds with explicit images and ideas, using their down time to meditate on these things. If a sexual thought enters their minds, they run with it.

If anyone suggests that this might be unhealthy or destructive to their souls, they might find ways to justify it. They mentally defend their actions with the argument that "I'm just a teenager, so I can't be expected to do otherwise."

Granted, if the details of these thoughts were put on display for the world to see, these guys would likely be horribly embarrassed. It just goes to show that most guys know their private sexual thoughts aren't healthy, but they nurture them anyway.

This is where most guys begin to get hooked into sexual sin. They don't learn to control their thoughts and they eventually start habitually doing things that they later regret but often can't easily control. For most young men today, that's probably going to involve looking at porn on the internet. More on that in the next chapter.

## HOW YOU CAN BE DIFFERENT

One of the keys to having an awesome life is simple peace of mind. It's what you experience when you are in a right relationship with God and the people around you. It's the "ahhhhh" feeling you get when your head hits the pillow at night. It comes when your private life lines up pretty well with your public life.

Most guys don't experience this kind of peace because their private thoughts are a whole lot more ugly than what they show on the outside. But you can choose to be different from that. As you submit your thought life to God and make a commitment to guarding your heart, you'll find the inner contentment and "abundant life" that God wants you to have. (See John 10:10.)

Make no mistake. This requires work. It requires focus. Your idle, wandering mind can easily go to dark places. You have to train it to think good thoughts and dream God-honoring dreams. But it can be done. Even so, it will be something that you will have to wrestle with all the days of your life.

## FROM THE LIFE OF DAVID

The story of David's life is found mainly in I Samuel, II Samuel and I Kings. But the book of Psalms is also a big collection of the songs he wrote. Because he was typically a raw and honest songwriter, you can read the Psalms to gain some insight into David's life and feelings.

David's thought life was certainly a source of struggle. In Psalm 13:2a, he questions God: *"How long must I wrestle with my thoughts and day after day have sorrow in my heart?"* He compares controlling his mind to a wrestling match: it is challenging and violent. Many days the fight left him with sorrow and pain.

In Psalm 55:2, David reflects, *"My thoughts trouble me and I am distraught."* He was probably ashamed of some of the things he thought. It robbed him of the peace of mind that we all need in life. Can you relate? I sure can.

But instead of denying that he had impure or troubling thoughts, he was willing to confront them head-on. Instead of trying to hide them, he brought them directly to God. In Psalm 26:2, he writes, *"Test me, LORD, and try me; examine my heart and mind."*

He was aware that God already knew his every thought. So, instead of trying to keep the ugly parts of his mind from God, David invited Him to help. He asked God to show him the darkness in his heart that even he wasn't aware of yet. Only then could he start to confront the stuff that was there.

How you think and what you think about have the power to dictate how you live. Beyond the potential for all sorts of impure sexual thoughts (that lead to all sorts of issues we will talk about in the next chapters), there are the thoughts you have about yourself.

What you think about who you are can ultimately define your life. Do you see yourself as capable? Lovable? Worthy? Valued? Guys who regularly entertain thoughts of inadequacy or worthlessness have a hard time facing the challenges of life with confidence. In contrast, guys who have a healthy self-esteem do much better.

You need to believe that God loves you and has a plan for your life. Unfortunately, most guys struggle with believing this during the teenage years. Because there are so many unknowns, it's easy for your mind to start believing that you don't matter or that your life won't ever amount to much.

Because of how destructive these thoughts can be, you have to start aggressively reeling in your thought life.

## TAKE ACTION

These action steps might seem a little preachy, but I promise that they are also very practical. Do these things and you will be on your way to making your thoughts your ally instead of your enemy.

### 1. Take every thought captive.

Every thought you have will either build you up or knock you down. They will either draw you closer to God and His awesome plans for your life or move you away from Him. That's why 2 Corinthians 10:5b tells you to *take captive every thought to make it obedient to Christ.*

Be wise enough to evaluate your thoughts and deliberately reject those that don't align with God's best for you. When something enters your mind that isn't good, treat it like a hostile prisoner; capture it, handcuff it, and beat the snot out of it. Be ruthless in this! Ask God for His help and He WILL help you. You know you don't have what it takes to do this on your own.

## 2. "Feed your dog."

There is a good dog and a bad dog inside the heart of every young man. The one you feed is the one that lives. Almost every action of your heart and mind serves to feed one of the dogs. Romans 8:5 addresses these two dogs directly, *"Those who live according to the flesh have their minds set on what the flesh desires; but those who live in accordance with the Spirit have their minds set on what the Spirit desires."*

The Bible calls these two dogs "flesh" and "Spirit." One is what you want; the other is what God wants. Make choices every day that feed one dog and starve the other one. Over time, God's Spirit in you will grow strong and the fleshy parts of you will grow weak.

## 3. Focus on God more than your sin.

Some people place so much focus on NOT sinning that they grow tired and weak in the fight. They end up sinning anyway. A better way is to focus on God and His power so that the sin loses its power over you. Galatians 5:16 puts it like this, *"Walk by the Spirit, and you will not gratify the desires of the flesh."*

A young man who actively walks with God will find it much more difficult to walk in sin. As you talk to God and meditate on His

Word, your mind will change. Your thoughts will move away from the junk and towards the things of God.

If you're going to build a life of awesomeness, you have to start with your thought life. That means aggressively guarding what you put in your mind. When your thoughts are overly critical of yourself, you need to replace them with how God sees you. (He thinks you are pretty amazing.) When your mind wanders towards impure thoughts about girls, you need to take your thoughts somewhere else.

> "Sow a thought, reap an action; sow an action, reap a habit; sow a habit, reap a character; sow a character, reap a destiny."
> –Stephen Covey

Just like the slow creation of a stalagmite in a cave, you are slowly establishing the person that you are. Your life will likely be made up of 30,000 days (more or less), but you need to know that what you do on this day matters. What you *think about* today matters.

Watch a great video called "Chapter 2 – Terry Crews " at www.infoforfamilies.com/awesome. In it, Terry talks about how his thought life got him into trouble.

# TALK ABOUT IT:

1. Who do you know whose life didn't turn out like they hoped because of a lifetime of bad thoughts and decisions? Where do you suppose they went wrong?

2. Have you ever struggled with thoughts that made you feel shame or guilt? How do you manage them wisely? In what ways do you manage them poorly?

3. What specific steps can you take to begin to train your mind to align with God's best for your life? How can you feed the "good dog" and starve the "bad dog?"

When I inhale helium my voice gets deeper.

# 3. Protecting Your Eyes

*"Pornography really really messed up my life." – Terry Crews*

Watch "Chapter 3 – Protecting Your Eyes" at www.infoforfamilies.com/awesome.

I told you from the beginning of this that we were going to talk honestly about some issues that have the power to destroy your life. This is where we start getting very specific.

For generations, men have been drawn to porn. Your father and your grandfather were probably curious about it as teenagers. They probably looked at it when they had the chance. The problem is that they rarely had the chance.

For your grandfather's generation, it meant going to a public movie theater in the bad part of town. He would have to buy a ticket and sit in a theater with a bunch of other guys and watch naked people on the big screen. Creepy.

When your dad was a teenager, he had to get hold of an "adult magazine." Playboy was the go-to choice. These were hard to find. Your dad can probably tell you a few stories of finding one at a friend's house. At the time, he probably felt like he struck it rich.

But things are different today. Technology gives your generation easy and private access to all the porn you want. For the past 20 years, computers have brought porn directly into our homes. For the past five, smartphones have brought it into our pockets. Young people are seeing more porn than any generation in history.

> Porn sites get more traffic than Netflix,
> Amazon and Twitter combined.

The most recent research suggests that the vast majority of teenage guys are in the habit of looking at online porn. (If you're not, you would be wise to keep it that way.) The data of how this behavior is impacting the young men around you is troubling, to say the least.

Porn is fundamentally changing the way men think about women and sex. I have seen this first-hand in working with the first generation of men who have grown up with easy access to it. For the past decade, I worked at a large church with young married couples. I have coached literally hundreds of newlywed men in their young twenties. Most of them are good guys with good intentions. They love Jesus and they love their wives. But most of them have spent the past decade looking at porn.

As they tell me their stories, I hear the same basic thing over and over again, "Before I got married, I didn't fool around with girls much. But, I looked at a lot of porn. Then, I fell in love and got married. I was thrilled that I finally had an outlet for my sexual desires and that porn wouldn't be a problem anymore. But I was wrong. I still find myself looking at it. I just can't stop."

Today, 56% of divorce cases involve one of the spouses having an obsession with online porn. Just 10 years ago, porn was almost never mentioned as a cause of marriage failure.

I wouldn't bring this up if everyone's stories weren't so similar. The choices you make regarding what you see as a young man have the power to impact you throughout your lifetime. That's why it's so important to take this seriously and confront it head-on.

# THE BIG IDEA:

## Porn has the power to destroy your life.

God made you with both the desire and the ability to connect sexually with a woman. That woman is your wife. Sex in marriage is an amazing and mind-blowing thing. It is absolutely worth waiting for.

But as we shared earlier, the enemy of God is committed to screwing that up in your life. Satan wants to sell you on a counterfeit version of sex that isn't nearly as satisfying or rewarding. In our culture today, porn is his tool of choice.

It's interesting that premarital sex among teenagers is actually on the decline today. This has happened because porn has taken its place. And while it promises to enhance sex, it is actually ruining it. Literally ruining it.

In March of 2016, Time magazine ran a cover story about the impact of porn on young men. They talked to a bunch of guys in their 20's and examined a ton of research on how porn was impacting their sexuality. Do you know what they found? Habitual porn use made many guys unable to function sexually.

> Can you believe that we live in a world where "Porn Induced Erectile Dysfunction" is actually a thing? Twenty year old guys needing to take Viagra...it's unbelievable.

Their brains were overwhelmed with the catalogue of sexual images that their eyes had seen. When they tried to have sex with a real person, their bodies wouldn't respond. The circuits in their brain designed to trigger arousal were fried. This can happen to married guys just as it happens to single guys.

Then you have to consider the addictive power of this stuff. Some scientists say it's worse than cocaine and heroin. In fact, some equate it to a one-two punch of both those drugs: it triggers an "upper" response when you're browsing. Then a "downer" response when masturbation is involved. (More on that in the next chapter.)

Youth culture expert Chap Clark says that more than 60% of teenage guys in America are addicted to porn. That means more than half of your friends are in literal bondage to the stuff. Many more than that see it as a major fight. I'm no math whiz, but the odds are pretty good that you see this as a struggle in your own life, as well.

There's one more scientific thing to consider. Porn actually has the power to change the way your brain works and functions. I could go into detail on this, but there's a great video put out by FightTheNewDrug.org that does a terrific job of explaining it. (You'll find it at the end of this chapter.)

# So let's consider what we know:

## 1. Porn diminishes a man's sexual response.
## 2. Porn is as addictive as any drug.
## 3. Porn rewires you brain in some very negative ways.

Beyond all that, you would be wise to consider the words of Jesus. In His most well-known sermon, he reminds you that the attitude of your heart is far more important than your external behavior. When talking about sexual sin, Jesus said the following:

*"You have heard that it was said, 'You shall not commit adultery.' But I tell you that anyone who looks at a woman lustfully has already committed adultery with her in his heart."* (Matthew 5: 27-28)

Let's be very clear. Porn is not entertainment. It is not recreation. It is sin. It has the power to destroy your life on many different levels. And perhaps most significantly, it is the biggest thing that Satan will use to get young men feeling powerless and unusable by God. This is NOT awesome.

## LISTEN TO YOUR BODY
# "WE ARE YOUR EYES."

To be honest, we have a tendency to wander. We are naturally drawn to stuff like explosions and viral videos. The problem is that everything you run past us gets filed away in your mind. That is especially true for sexual images. Over your lifetime, you build something of a "visual hard drive" of all the stuff we have seen. Unfortunately, once something is saved, it's really hard to delete. That's why it's so important to make wise choices regarding what you let us see.

# HOW MOST GUYS OPERATE

You need to realize from the get-go that most guys see porn as the norm. To them, it's not a big deal. Everybody does it. But they don't realize how it is changing how they think about sex and about the women around them.

They are unconsciously learning that women are to be used. Over time they will come to see them as one-dimensional, as physical beings with the purpose of gratifying a man's sexual needs. They have a hard time considering a girl's emotional, relational, and spiritual dimensions. These guys are missing out on a lot.

> Learning about sex by watching porn is like learning to drive by playing Mario Kart. It's so far removed from reality that it's not even helpful.

Most guys think that watching porn is helping them to learn about sex. This is ridiculous. Porn is a counterfeit, version of something significant. People who make porn don't behave like real people in love relationships do. Guys think they are getting a leg up in understanding how sex works but what they are actually doing is handicapping themselves. These guys enter marriage one day ill-equipped to make love to and connect in meaningful ways with their wives.

# HOW YOU CAN BE DIFFERENT

You know that porn is toxic and addictive.
You know that it has the power and potential to do serious damage to your life, your relationships, and your walk with God. So you can take drastic measures to keep your eyes far from it.

You can commit to being a "one woman kind of man." While this will likely be impossible to carry out perfectly, you can make it your goal to see one naked woman in your lifetime. Of course, that would be your wife. God created a lot of beautiful "Eves" out there, but you need to save your looks for the one Eve that God will bring to you one day.

Beyond guarding your own eyes, you can strive to be a young man who helps others find victory in this fight. You know that your friends struggle with this, so you should be willing to take the initiative to push your peers towards purity. Most guys are looking for someone to walk through this battle with them. You can be that person.

# FROM THE LIFE OF DAVID

While we know David as a hero, he was definitely a flawed one. One of his biggest mistakes was not guarding his eyes. It got him into the biggest trouble of his life.

In II Samuel 11:2-4 we find the story: *"One evening David got up from his bed and walked around on the roof of the palace. From the roof he saw a woman bathing. The woman was very beautiful, and David sent someone to find out about her. The man said, "She is Bathsheba, the daughter of Eliam and the wife of Uriah the Hittite." Then David sent messengers to get her. She came to him, and he slept with her."*

Picture this: David is on his roof, minding his own business, when his eyes land on a beautiful woman taking a bath. Instead of looking away, he allows his mind to wander towards a lustful place. Then he takes things a deliberate step further by having the woman brought to his home so he could have sex with her.

This led to a pregnancy, a murder, and all sorts of other problems. It just proves that what seems harmless at the time can easily snowball into something much more disastrous in your life.

Even though he lived thousands of years ago, there is a practical principle you can learn from David's screw up.

It is related to the power a king has over all that he rules.

Your eyes are probably not going to get you into trouble on the rooftop of your palace, but they can easily get you into trouble via your smartphone, tablet or computer. So here's the principle: Just as David was king over his kingdom, you are the king of your devices. Consider the following chart:

| David and His Rule: | You and Your Phone: |
|---|---|
| *His subjects did exactly what he told them. | *You phone does exactly what you tell it to do. |
| *When he saw Bathsheba, he could have told his soldiers to remove her from the roof. | *When you are tempted to look at porn, you can remove your phone from view. |
| *He could have declared a law: "Nobody can get naked on their roof from now on." | *You can set up blocks and filters that don't allow it to show naked people. |
| *He could have had his close advisors check in on him regularly. | *You can welcome accountability from your parents. |

You have great power over your phone and the other technology in your life. While the temptation can be overwhelming at times, you are ultimately responsible for the consequences when you look at porn. You are the one who has to do something about it. Nobody is going to do this work for you.

# TAKE ACTION

When Jesus talked about a man's tendency to lust, he offered a rather extreme suggestion on how to deal with it. In Matthew 5:29 he said, *"If your right eye causes you to stumble, gouge it out and throw it away. It is better for you to lose one part of your body than for your whole body to be thrown into hell."* While we don't take this literally (please keep your eyes in your head), we can know that we need to take this fight very seriously. Here are some more practical steps to take:

## 1. Safeguard your technology.

Just as David could have done, you need to command your devices to do the right things to protect your eyes. If your family doesn't use some kind of internet filter or tracking software on your technology, insist that you get some. Welcome it as a gift from God and gladly submit to it.

## 2. Bring the struggle to God.

When you're looking at stuff you shouldn't be looking at, your natural tendency is to hide it. Do it long enough, and you'll start believing a lie: "You're a disappointment to God, so don't bother going to Him right now." The truth is that God knows and sees all. You can't hide from Him. He wants to help you with the struggle, but He can't if you keep (foolishly) keeping it from Him.

Instead, invite Him into the fight. When you are tempted, talk to Him. Quote His Word. Cry out for help. Just don't try to hide. He knows what you're doing and He still loves you. Jesus has seen (and paid for) the ugliest sins that the world can commit, so He's not shocked by what you are capable of. Running away from Him is the worst thing you can do.

## 3. Build some new skills.

There's some bad news: you're likely going to struggle with this until the day you die. So, if sexual temptation is always going to be there, you're going to need some tools to fight it. In his book, *Every Man's Battle*, Steven Arterburn offers a few habits you need to build into your life.

Start by learning to "bounce your eyes." In the course of any given day, you're going to see sexual images on your computer and the TV. You're going to interact with women who are showing too much skin. You can't help see it, but your immediate response should be to bounce your eyes and look somewhere else. Move away quickly. The longer you stay, the more your thoughts take you to places you don't need to go.

This skill was established in scripture long before Arterburn dreamed it up. In Job 31:1, he declares, *"I made a covenant with my eyes not to look lustfully at a young woman."* Job's commitment can be your commitment. In fact, that might be a good Bible verse for you to memorize.

## 4. Tell somebody.

While you can be tempted to keep your private sins in the dark, it's actually the worst thing you can do. When you bring this stuff into the light, it's much easier to deal with. In many ways, it loses it's power in your life. Plus, you're no longer alone.

One of the best things you can do to overcome this is to share your struggle with someone you trust. I promise that if you talk to another guy about this, he's not going to judge you. He's going to relate. And if you share it with someone who is further along in life (more mature) than you are, he will likely give you some support and encouragement. You need this. We all need this.

Every young man knows the reality of this struggle. Sadly, some men get so addicted to porn that they require inpatient treatment. Sadder still, those numbers are growing. Porn is the modern-day plague that is devastating the men of your generation. You can't afford to relax and treat it lightly.

Take whatever steps you need to create some accountability and to build some new habits. Guarding your eyes takes constant discipline and you can't ever get lazy. But also choose to walk in God's grace. He loves you, even when you blow it. In those dark moments, run towards Him, not away from Him. He can handle your sin. The cross assures you of that reality.

To learn about the impact of porn on your brain, watch the video called "Chapter 3 – We Need to Talk" at www.infoforfamilies.com/awesome.

# TALK ABOUT IT:

1. Is this an area of struggle for you? For your peers? When did it start? When did it become a serious temptation for you (if ever)?

2. Why is it so hard to talk about this temptation openly with other guys? Why do we need to?

3. What specific steps are you going to take to protect your eyes in the coming days?

Third degree burns? Good,
I needed some new skin.

# 4. Killing your Selfishness

*"I don't want to tell your story because you're an insensitive, self-centered moron." - Director Joel Schumacher*

Watch the video called "Chapter 4 – Killing Your Selfishness" at www.infoforfamilies.com/awesome.

What do you love? What is something in your life that might be insignificant in the grand scheme of things, but that you truly love? There are probably lots of things (some of them sort of stupid) that come to mind.

For me, the first thing that comes to mind is guacamole. I love guacamole. That wonderful combination of avocados, onions, spices, etc. is what makes Mexican food work. If I'm ordering a burrito at Chipotle and I'm a few dollars short and can't afford to add the guacamole (it's extra, you know), I can start to tear up. I seriously consider borrowing money from strangers. I absolutely love guacamole.

Something else that I love is my wife. We've done life together for more than a quarter century, so we have shared experiences, memories, and goals. She's my partner and my "other half" so, of course, I love her.

Here we see a great example of the limitations of the English language. I can use the same word to describe my commitment to my spouse that I use to describe a condiment that I put on my burrito. One is a selfless devotion. The other is a self-satisfying preference.

Unfortunately, this self-centered concept of "love" has found its way into romantic relationships within our culture. When I am coaching an engaged couple, I will often ask the guy, "Why do you love your girl?" Here are the most common answers I get:

1. She makes me happy.
2. She meets my needs.
3. She's everything I ever dreamed of in a wife.
4. She brings out the best in me.

While these answers sound nice and romantic, I want you to notice something about them. They are all self-centered. At the root of them are the words "me," "my," and "I." It's as if the guy is saying, *"Who I really love is me. This woman enhances my life; she makes it better. As long as she does that, then I will love her."*

For too many young people, "love" has become a selfish endeavor instead of a sacrificial one. It's because we have trained ourselves to think of ourselves and forget what real love looks like.

# TRUE LOVE TEST:

Here's a good way to see if you really "love" a girl. Consider how you feel about her long-term if she can no longer do the things that make you "love" her. Maybe she has an accident and loses body or brain function. She can't meet your needs or give anything to the relationship. Are you still in love with her? For how long?

Real love is radically different than "guacamole" love. It is demonstrated perfectly by God. He loves you no matter what. Even if you don't love Him back, His love is extravagant, sacrificial, and never-ending. He loves you consistently, even if He never gets anything in return.

Real love is rooted in what you do for another, not in how another makes you feel. It is best characterized in what is known as "the love chapter" in the Bible. Paul writes this in I Corinthians 13:4-5: *Love is patient, love is kind. It does not envy, it does not boast, it is not proud. It does not dishonor others, it is not self-seeking, it is not easily angered, it keeps no record of wrongs."*

Note that true love has nothing to do with emotions but everything to do with sacrifice. When you begin to embrace the idea of selflessness as your model for how to love, you can start moving towards a life of awesomeness. As God transforms your heart, you begin to see sacrifice and generosity as key factors in how you love others. This is especially true for how you will love your wife someday.

# THE BIG IDEA:

## A self-centered life is an empty life.

So why are we talking about selfishness in these early chapters about guarding your heart? We've already considered the impact of your thought life and the importance of protecting your eyes from looking at porn. But we are going to take things one step further. There is a key application of your natural tendency to be selfish as it relates to your sexuality.

For many men, sex is a self-centered experience. It is a way to meet their own needs and they will use whatever woman they can "hook up" with to make it happen. With most men, this selfish motive was hard-wired into their brains long before they started having sex. It started with a habit of masturbation. They discovered that they could touch themselves and experience sexual release. It was quick, easy, and self-gratifying.

---

Here's another disorder: **Chronic Masturbatory Syndrome**
is when a grown man can't perform sexually because he has
trained his body to only respond to his own hand.
Personally, this is something that I want to avoid.

---

In God's design – the way He made things to work – sex is an interpersonal act. You bond with another person (ideally your wife), giving yourself to her for her benefit...her pleasure. Porn and masturbation have flipped this around and made it purely a self-satisfying act for an entire generation of men.

You know that dopamine release that your brain gives you when it experiences pleasure? You get that when you masturbate. But, if you do it long enough and frequently enough, it has the power to overwhelm and fry the circuits in your brain, making it hard for your brain to connect properly in a relationship. Your brain is literally trained to be selfish. You forget that sex is primarily given, not taken.

That's why it is so important to consider this stuff now instead of later. What you do as a teenager truly has the power to impact the rest of your life. If you hope to one day make a meaningful connection with a girl, you need to practice being selfless. Masturbation takes you in the opposite direction.

## LISTEN TO YOUR BODY
# "WE ARE YOUR HANDS."

You discovered us when you first put us in your mouth at about 3 months old. (Thanks for that disgusting experience, by the way.) As a young man, you have us so that you can build and serve. So that you can use us to add value to the lives of other people. So how are you using your hands? Are you being generous or selfish with them? For the record, masturbation is probably the most selfish thing you can do with us.

# HOW MOST GUYS OPERATE

Masturbation has become normalized to your generation. "Everybody does it," is a rallying cry. And, while most studies suggest that the vast majority of young men do it, there used to be a sense of shame around it. No more. Now, it is celebrated.

For many young men it becomes a habit, an addiction. What these guys don't realize is how it is affecting their minds and bodies. And most young guys don't realize how it will impact their long-term relationships. I have seen this devastation in many young marriages.

I have seen guys in their twenties who marry beautiful girls. After a while, these guys discover that their wives require something of them for sex to work right. The guys have to love, romance, and connect emotionally with their girls. They have to give themselves away and sacrifice their wants and desires to meet their wives' needs. This is necessary and normal in any healthy marriage.

Pause for a second to watch "Chapter 4 - Porn's Impact on Marriage" at www.infoforfamilies.com/ awesome. It will help you better understand what I'm talking about.

Newly married guys who have a strong history of porn use and masturbation grow weary of sacrificial love rather quickly. Their patterns of behavior through their teen and young adult years have made them lazy. They have grown selfish. Their sexual minds have been trained to ask: "What's in it for me?"

Sex has become something designed for their pleasure, not as a way to demonstrate love for another person. Because of this self-centered attitude, they miss out on an essential and rewarding part of what marriage was designed to be.

While this might seem like a rare occurrence, my experience is that it is becoming all too common. The marriages of your generation are being negatively impacted by this one factor more than just about anything else.

# HOW YOU CAN BE DIFFERENT

You're going to be different from most guys. You are going to spend your teen years learning what it means to be selfless, knowing that you'll desperately need that skill in marriage. A big part of this will be fighting the temptation to meet your own sexual needs. You will see your sexuality as a gift to be given. It is a gift that one day your wife will give to you. It is not something that you should practice taking for yourself.

You need to know how important this is. God takes the sin of lust very seriously. But you also need to remember that God offers you grace and forgiveness when you mess up. And you will probably mess up along the way. Don't be so tough on yourself that you forget that God still loves you. The enemy will dump guilt and shame on you in an attempt to get you to hide from God. Don't do it. Run back to God and choose to walk in His better way.

Having victory over this struggle will never be easy. But it can be done. God can and will help you to guard your heart, your mind ,and even your body.

# FROM THE LIFE OF DAVID

The first story most kids probably learned about David was his fight with Goliath. You know the one. Everyone else in God's army was scared of this giant of a bully. Nobody would fight him. But David boldly volunteered, even though he was just a teen. (You can find the story in I Samuel 17.)

David faced Goliath armed with just a rock and a sling. After a little God-inspired smack talk, David knocked Goliath out with a direct hit to the forehead. Then, while the giant was dazed on the ground, David used Goliath's enormous sword to chop the guy's head clean off. This is definitely one of those biblical scenes rated "R" for extreme violence.

While this story has nothing to do with masturbation, it does give you a good example of how you deal with your enemy. (And let's be clear: habitually looking at images and pleasuring yourself is the mortal enemy of your heart and soul.) So what can we learn?

David dealt with his enemy directly. When the other men around him were passive and cowardly, he was aggressive and straightforward. He boldly stepped in to the fight, asked for God's help, and subdued the threat. Then he chopped his enemy's head off.

When it comes to your heart, your self-centered desires will always be fighting for control of your life. But know this: selfishness will always lead to isolation. The very things that you think will make you happy are usually the things that will cause you pain and grief.

That's why Jesus was clear in Luke 9:24 when He called you to a life of awesomeness, *"For whoever wants to save their life will lose it, but whoever loses their life for me will save it."* It's totally counter-intuitive. Getting yourself out of the way and prioritizing the needs of others are at the foundation of a great life.

You must come to see selfishness as an enemy of your life. Just as David cut off his enemy's head, you must be equally aggressive in killing off your selfish tendencies. You must treat sexual sin as a giant who is out to kill you. You also must remember that God is on your side. The giant doesn't stand a chance.

# TAKE ACTION

A better suggestion here would be to choose *inaction*, to NOT take part in a self-centered practice that is bad for your body and soul. But here are a few key steps you can take to keep a bad habit out of your life:

## 1. Make a decision.

Whether you are 12 or 20, you can choose RIGHT NOW to have an opinion about porn and masturbation. You can know that it has a negative effect on your heart, your body, and your relationships. Most importantly, you can make a commitment to abstain. No matter what you have done up to this point, you can draw a line in the sand today. Ask your friends to hold you accountable to this and commit to doing the same for them.

## 2. Reprogram your brain.

If this has been a regular part of your life for a while, it can be hard to stop. Like any other addiction, your brain has been programmed to want to keep on doing it. Parts of your circuitry have been damaged, and it might take a while to get them moving in a healthy way again. This might take some real effort but it can be done. Know that God wants to help you. Cry out to Him often and keep Him and His word close to you at all times.

> **Brain Buddy** is a smartphone app that is designed to help men to reprogram their brains from sexual addiction.

## 3. Practice sacrificial love.

While you're not married yet, you will probably want to be one day. If you are choosing not to practice selfish love during your teen years, you might as well start learning how to love a girl in a sacrificial way. Ephesians 5:25 commands husbands to *"love your wives, just as Christ loved the church and gave Himself up for her."*

Every day, you will have opportunities to love the women in your life (your mom, sisters, friends, etc.) in ways that model Christ. Sacrifice your wants and needs to meet the needs of the other gender in big and small ways whenever you have the chance. I promise, they will think you are awesome.

I hate that we have had to explore these issues in such explicit detail in these first few chapters. But they are the battlefields where so many young men are struggling in the fight...and losing.

If you can't walk in victory in these areas, then it becomes much harder to walk in victory in the other areas of your relational and spiritual life. Too many good young men are suffering internally because they feel defeated in the private and secret parts of their lives.

But if you can get this right – if you can be diligent to guard your heart and protect your eyes and your mind from all the junk that is available to you – your life will be radically different from most guys out there. You will be better prepared to start tackling the next big goals for your life: getting the girl and saving the world.

Take a moment to pray, asking God to help you to experience real victory in this area of your life. Remember, He promises to help you along the way.

Watch the encouraging video called "Chapter 4 – Nick's Story" at www.infoforfamilies.com/awesome.

# TALK ABOUT IT:

1. If you have never masturbated before, that's a very good thing. What motivates you not to start?

2. Can you see the connection between self-stimulation and self-centered love? How do you think that frequent masturbation could leave you poorly prepared for marriage?

3. What are some practical ways (both big and small) that you can sacrificially serve the women in your life?

There's no such thing as strong coffee. Just weak people.

# 5. Getting a Girlfriend

*"Being in a relationship with no intent to marry is like going to the grocery store with no money. You either leave unhappy or take something that isn't yours." – Jefferson Bethke*

Watch "Chapter 5 – Getting a Girlfriend" at www.infoforfamilies.com/awesome.

Tucked away in the heart of just about every young man is the desire to share his life with a young woman. At some point in your journey from childhood to adulthood, this desire will be awakened. If it hasn't happened yet, just wait. It's just around the corner.

God puts this in your heart. From as early as the 2nd chapter of Genesis, God declared that *"It is not good for man to be alone."* He dreamed up woman as a perfect complement to man. Then he wired you to notice her beauty and her feminine qualities. He also wired you to desire her sexually.

From what you read in the last few chapters, you would think that this desire is a bad thing. But it's very good. It just needs to be controlled and focused into the correct place, your future wife. Managing it between now and then requires a great deal of discipline.

That's why it's worth talking about getting a girlfriend and when the right time might be for that. There's not some magical age when entering a romantic relationship is right for every guy, but there are some things you should consider before you get there.

As we already discussed, you are going to have a tendency towards selfishness. This is true at some level for every guy. If they are honest, most of the reasons that guys give for wanting a girlfriend are rooted in this selfishness. At best, they want the girl's affection and commitment as a self-esteem boost. (She loves me!) At worst, they want an outlet for their sexual desires. Nobody talks about this, but it's true.

Here's the bad news about that. When you bring your (unintentional) selfishness into a relationship, it's bad practice for marriage. And that's what most romantic relationships among teenagers end up being: bad, self-centered rehearsal for how marriage will work. You're usually operating with "what can you do for me" motives. This undermines everything that God made your marriage to one day become.

When you add to that the emotions of "love" and your newfound sexual drive, things can get out of hand very quickly. A sweet and innocent relationship can turn sexual quicker than you expect. It can be more than the typical teenager is equipped to deal with.

It is like giving plutonium to a preschooler and telling him to go play with it in the backyard. He's just not equipped or ready to handle it with the care that is needed. And while nuclear materials certainly require an intense level of safekeeping, the reality is that most boyfriend/girlfriend relationships are equally as fragile.

# THE BIG IDEA:

## Don't enter a relationship until you are ready.

You might enter a relationship with a girl with every intention of it not turning physical, but rarely does that hold up. Any relationship that is moving deeper and deeper emotionally has the potential to get out of control physically.

In 7th grade, I was fully committed to purity. In 8th and 9th grade...I was still in. By 10th grade, I was to the point of looking down on those I knew who were being promiscuous in their relationships. I thought, "Why would someone be so foolish as to compromise their sexual purity at such a young age?"

But in 11th grade, I got a serious girlfriend and something changed in me. Suddenly, my purity commitment was forgotten. The faithful desire to honor God with my body was trumped by my emotional affections for my girlfriend. While there were certain physical lines I was committed to not crossing, I know that the relationship was far from God-honoring.

Was there conflict within me? Of course. Those high school years were some of the most tumultuous in my Christian life.

Unfortunately, my desire for Christian obedience didn't stop me from becoming physical in ways that I know were sinful.

This can happen to any guy whose heart is turned toward a girl. That's why you have to move with great care when you start thinking about pursuing a relationship.

> You should be ready before you enter a serious relationship, but that doesn't mean that all dating is off the table. Taking a girl (who is a friend) to a dance with a larger group can be a great opportunity to practice being a gentleman. Just don't turn it into a big "Facebook official" deal.

## LISTEN TO YOUR BODY
# "WE ARE YOUR HORMONES."

A vital part of your body, we are driven from the pituitary gland near your brain and we dictate much of how your body functions. Oh, and we also have the potential to basically take control of your desires and behaviors. Because so many hormones that manage your sexuality kick in during your teens, we can be something of a shock to your system. You need to learn to manage us before you allow yourself to be controlled by us.

# HOW MOST GUYS OPERATE

Most guys don't think about this stuff at all. They rarely consider that getting a girlfriend and taking the relationship physical might be a bad thing. In fact, many treat this like a goal to achieve. This is rooted in three messages that the world around them is regularly communicating to them:

First, they believe that sexual activity is casual. It's no big deal. It is experienced as a normal, social part of a relationship. For some, it might not even include a relationship...it's just something you do with any girl who is willing. Sadly, there will always be girls willing to engage in sexual activity apart from any commitment. Thus, there will always be guys wanting to take advantage of them. (More on this later.)

Second, most guys believe that sex is essential. Sort of an illogical contradiction to the first thing above, they believe that sex is a huge deal. Some guys believe that if you're not sexually active in some way, you are weird and unhealthy. Saving sex for marriage is seen as unreasonable and just plain stupid. After all, they reason, sex is a natural act so you should let your body do what it wants to do.

> Studies show that most teenagers feel pressure to be in a relationship...to be sexually active. But most teenagers also say that their peers are in over their heads, entering relationships before they are emotionally mature.

Third, most guys think that sex is primarily physical. It is a biological urge that feels good. They divorce it from anything rooted in relationship and ignore the impact it has on their minds and emotions. There is little consideration for what the other person is feeling or thinking, instead seeing them as just a means to an end. If you have been paying attention, you can see how porn might fuel this type of thinking.

You can even see this shift in the modern music of your generation. In many songs referencing sex, the pronouns have changed from words like "her" to words like "it." Guys "hit this" or "get with that." They say "that body" instead of "you." It's as if sex is less about connecting with a person and more about a physical act. This thinking is both wrong and dangerous.

# HOW YOU CAN BE DIFFERENT

Because you know that sex is a big deal, you can be committed to both dating a girl and keeping things from getting physical. While other guys might take advantage of girls, you can be careful not to do that. That might sound like a good plan, but successfully pulling it off is always a bit harder than it seems. Again, that's why you shouldn't rush into it.

Several years ago, I had the chance to take a mission trip to Zambia, Africa. After a full week of ministry, we concluded our time with a road trip to Victoria Falls, the world's largest waterfall. With a width of more than a mile, the falls were like nothing I had ever seen before.

I rented some rain gear (because the water flow is like being in a thunderstorm) and walked alone to a place where I could get a good view. Carrying my camera in a plastic bag to keep it dry, I pulled it out to take a few pictures, but the angle from the trail I was on wasn't quite right. With no one to tell me not to, I climbed over the fence that marked the trail and climbed down a steep slope towards the Zambezi River, hoping to get a better look.

Finally, hanging over the side of a cliff I had the perfect view. I took a few pictures, feeling quite proud of myself. Then I looked around. I realized that I was alone, wearing rented flip flops, and standing on a steep, muddy slope with the river some 200 feet below me. One little slip climbing back up to the trail and I would tumble to my death. They would never find my body and nobody would ever know what happened to me. This realization inspired me to climb back up the hill with extreme care.

While I was still far above the river, safe from any danger, the slippery slope I was standing on had the power to take my life. In the same way, many guys think that their good intentions with their girlfriends will keep them far from sexual sin. But the truth is that one false move can leave them in a situation where they are in over their heads.

What you desperately need is a heart for God that compels you to stay on the trail and avoid any semblance of sexual sin. This is why you shouldn't start pursuing a girlfriend until you are mature enough to handle the temptations of the relationship. Only you can figure out when that is. (Your parents can help you. God probably has an opinion, too so keep Him in the loop.)

# FROM THE LIFE OF DAVID

When it came to pursuing girls, David was a terrible example. He had too many wives (more than one is too many), and that got him into trouble on more than one occasion.

But we can learn something from his son Solomon. His love life was put on clear display in the Song of Solomon, the song he "wrote" with his new wife. When you read it, it's like listening to a long duet that includes backup singers and everything.

Tucked within their song is a solid piece of advice that is custom-made for you. On three different occasions, the girl says, *"Do not arouse or awaken love until it so desires."* (Song of Solomon 2:7, 3:5, and 8:4)

The entire song describes the intense passion that lovers feel. (Remember, God created this.) It is like a wild beast that, once awakened, cannot be tamed. In that context, the lovers are both describing the powerful force that they now know AND they are warning their younger siblings to not go there until they are ready to handle it. Because once it is awakened, it is difficult to turn off.

*"Don't awaken love until you are ready."* This is good advice that you can't afford to ignore.

# How do you know if you're ready for a girlfriend?

There is not a perfect, exhaustive checklist for when you might be ready to enter a relationship, but here are some things to consider before you head down that road. If you can't say "YES" to all of the following questions, then you're probably not ready.

## 1. Is your identity rooted in Christ?

You need to know that your worth and identity is 100% defined by what God says about you. If you are looking for a girl to give you purpose or worth or value, you're looking in the wrong place. She's going to be a huge disappointment.

## 2. Is your main goal to serve the girl?

The Bible puts non-family women in your life into two categories: wives and sisters in Christ. There is nothing in-between those two. So are you willing to treat your girlfriend exactly like you treat your sister? She is not your physical and emotional play-toy. She is someone that you serve and help to become more like Jesus.

## 3. Are you willing to talk to the girl's father about it?

That girl you are interested in has a dad. He is ultimately responsible for her. This may sound old-fashioned, but if you want to take her out or pursue a relationship with her, you need to be willing to talk to him about it first. (As a dad, I wouldn't let you borrow my car without talking to me first. My daughters are a lot more valuable to me than my car is. So it makes sense that I would want to get to know you before you take my daughter out.) The dad might think it's odd, but it is very likely that he will appreciate it.

## 4. Can you break up in a healthy way?

If your relationship doesn't lead to marriage, it will eventually come to an end. Can you handle that? If you are ultimately rejected, can you move on without being emotionally devastated? Your response to number one above (about your identity in Christ) will help you to know the answer. Too many young people find their identity in their boyfriend/girlfriend relationship. When it ends, it feels like their lives are over. If you see your friends doing this, they aren't ready for a relationship.

## 5. Can you take sole responsibility for keeping the relationship sexually pure?

Our culture says that it's a girl's job to say "no" but that's just not true. You have to be the leader on this. Are you fully committed to that?

There are some who believe that you're not ready to date until you're ready to marry. That means you have the maturity and financial means to move quickly towards marriage. While that might seem a bit rigid (and way out in the future), there might be some wisdom there. Discuss some of these questions and parameters with an adult that you trust before you start pursuing a girl.

 ## TAKE ACTION

You may have started this chapter hoping that it would give you a step-by-step plan for getting a girlfriend. Sorry to disappoint you. Instead of rushing into a relationship, there are some clear things you can do to position yourself to get a girl at the right time:

## 1. Slow down.

While the guys around you might be actively seeking a girl to partner up with, take a big, deep breath and slow down. Don't feel obligated to join them. Most of the relationships your peers enter into during their teen years are shallow, pointless, and emotionally-taxing pursuits. They might not realize it at the time, but they will look back later with regret on what they did. I promise this is true.

## 2. Study the other gender.

Long before entering a relationship you can start figuring out what you like in a girl. Don't get creepy or anything, but observe what you like and value in the girls around you. Ask God to show you what character traits in a girl you will need through your life. Note that the right girl may not always be the prettiest or most popular. Proverbs 31:30a says, *"Charm is deceptive, and beauty is fleeting..."* Look for something deeper than just outward appearance.

## 3. Focus on growing up.

Too many guys are so worried about finding the right person that they forget to spend their developmental years becoming the right person. You have power over exactly one person in this world; so don't worry about finding someone who will "complete you." Instead, put your energies into growing up into the person that God wants you to be.

> "Do everything in your power to become the person who the person you're looking for is looking for." – Andy Stanley

There's one more thing to consider before you start dating. This is important (and deep), so do your best to take this in.

Don't evaluate the activities of your life based upon if they are "good or bad." If you do that with your romantic life, it's easy to conclude that having a girlfriend will be pretty good (or at least not too bad) and, therefore, worth doing. "Good or bad" is the wrong filter. You need something better than that.

If you are a follower of Christ, then your life exists for God's glory. The purpose of your life is to be in a relationship with God and to join Him in His plan to redeem the world. Period. If you have never heard this before, then let me be the first person to inform you of this reality.

Instead of asking if a relationship is "good" or "bad," a better question is to ask if a relationship will help you to more effectively fulfill God's purpose for your life. Will having a girlfriend at a given point better help you to walk with God and to serve Him with your life? Or will she be a distraction?

If they are honest, most Christian young men would admit that having a girlfriend would distract them from their pursuit of God. What about you? If having a girlfriend would move your energies and emotions towards the girl and away from God, then you're probably not ready. If the sexual temptation of being close to her will distract you from having a pure heart, then you're probably not ready.

One day, your time will come. You'll find the right girl who can join you on your pursuit of building an awesome life under God's leadership. She will be a "helpmate" to you and increase your capacity to do great things for the Kingdom. God will use her in unique ways to refine and mature you into the image of Christ.

That will happen eventually. And it will be incredible. In the meantime, keep becoming the man that God desires. Be willing to patiently wait for the right time when God will bring the right girl into your life.

Watch the video called "Chapter 5 - Jake's Story" at www.infoforfamilies.com/awesome.

# TALK ABOUT IT

1. Do you think most teenagers who are in romantic relationships are mature enough to handle them? Why or why not?

2. On a scale of 1 to 10, how difficult do you think it is to keep a relationship sexually pure? Why do you think that?

3. How can you know that you are ready to enter a relationship? What factors will it depend upon?

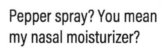

Pepper spray? You mean
my nasal moisturizer?

# 6. Understanding Your Sexual Chemistry

*"Sex makes you stupid." – Mark Gungor*

Watch "Chapter 6 – Understanding Your Sexual Chemistry" at www.infoforfamilies.com/awesome.

If you're going to be awesome, you need to know about a powerful little chemical called "oxytocin." As a drug, it has the potential to influence you more than alcohol, marijuana, and all other illegal substances combined. Unfortunately, most guys have never even heard of it.

Do a Google search for oxytocin and more than a million results will be available. Even better, search for something a little more specific to the issues we are considering here. Google "oxytocin teenagers sex connection." There is a lot to read.

Oxytocin is known by scientists as "the bonding chemical." It is secreted in the bodies of both men and women, helping to create meaningful bonds and attachments to others. When your body generates it, you feel emotionally connected to the person you are with. Oxytocin can be stimulated by something as simple as a really good hug with someone you love, but it really gets going during times of sexual intimacy.

God, who created everything, knew what He was doing when He created oxytocin. He created a powerful chemical bond that makes sex more than just a biological act. It is why I have heard sex referred to as the "super glue of marriage." It binds a husband and wife together in a way that is unique to all other human relationships.

Oxytocin plays a big part in this connection. It's the reason that God tells us to wait until marriage to have sex. In the context of pre-marital sexual activity, oxytocin has the power to undermine the very thing that it was designed to do, as this magical stuff doesn't know if the people who are secreting it are in a marriage relationship or not. It bonds any couple of any age experiencing sexual intimacy.

# THE BIG IDEA:

## Sex connects two people at a molecular level.

When it comes to what oxytocin does and how it works, there is some bad news and there is some good news. It all relates to how you connect with girls and how you will eventually connect with your wife. You would be wise to understand what it does to you.

# Here's The Bad News:

The bad news is that sex makes you stupid. Specifically, sexual activity outside of marriage has the potential to make you feel crazy in love with a girl, even if she's not the right girl for you. All the time, guys confuse lust with love and oxytocin serves as the fuel that powers their stupidity. There's no denying it: the physical dimensions of a boy/girl relationship will mask the flaws in every other part of the relationship.

Even if the sexual activity is relatively benign - passionate kissing, for example - there is a biological component at work beneath the surface. It's like an addict who keeps going back to a drug that is bad for him. Young couples who are "hooked" on one another can consistently overlook the troubling parts of their relationship and stay together regardless. This can last indefinitely or until one of them finally hits a wall (or notices someone else) and ends the relationship.

The "bad news" of oxytocin is that you end up bonding with the wrong people. And, unfortunately, it negatively affects your ability to bond in marriage.

> Studies have shown if you have multiple physical relationships that then break up, you weaken your ability to form a long-term commitment.

Several studies suggest that the greatest predictor of divorce is the number of previous sexual partners a person has before they marry. The more they have, the greater the chance of divorce. Again, what happens before marriage has big impact.

# Here's The Good News:

The "good news" of oxytocin is that it is a key part of God's plan to build unbelievable strength in your marriage relationship someday. Here's how it is designed to work:

Take two virgins with limited sexual experience. Let them develop a slow-simmering emotional connection based upon self-sacrificing love as modeled by Christ. Eventually, get them to an altar where, in front of their family, all their best friends, and a holy God, they pledge their lives and their all to one another. Then, safely in their marriage bed and with God's blessing, they have their first sexual experiences with one another. In this scenario, they are powerfully imprinting emotionally on each other, not just on the sexual act. The oxytocin that God created to connect two people overwhelms them for one another.

Considered in this light, God's command to save sexual activity for marriage is less of a downer and more of a blessing. He is purposely encouraging you to have the best sex possible – sex that perfectly ties emotional, spiritual, and physical intimacy together.

---

One study found that having just one other intimate relationship prior to marriage is linked to an increased risk of divorce.

---

As a young man looking to find God's best, you will be wise to know that there is chemical component to the *two become one* dynamic that the Bible talks about in Genesis 2:24, Matthew 19:5, and Ephesians 5:31. God is not trying to keep you from something. He is trying to protect you from messing up what He designed to be amazing in your marriage someday.

We can see that specific caution in I Corinthians 6:16 when Paul writes: *"Do you not know that he who unites himself with a prostitute is one with her in body? For it is said, 'The two will become one flesh.'"* God gives us clear directives about handling sexual intimacy (and our oxytocin) with great care.

He knows that sex will one day serve as superglue in your marriage. What is designed for your good in that relationship will do just the opposite in every other relationship. That's the reason that God tells you save sex for marriage.

## LISTEN TO YOUR BODY
# "WE ARE THE MOLECULES THAT MAKE UP YOUR BODY."

Listen to us! Oxytocin works at something of a molecular level. When you have sexual contact – even when it's something tame, like kissing – it causes every one of us to long for and connect with the girl. God designed you (and the girl) that way. But when the girl isn't your wife, this oxytocin bond can cause some pretty serious problems. Please, let us save our chemical connections for the girl you will marry one day.

# HOW MOST GUYS OPERATE

Most young people don't understand the logic of God's command to save sex for marriage. Sure, they may know God's opinion on the subject, but when sexual desire begins to awaken within them and they find themselves emotionally connected in a relationship, it's hard to remain convinced. With all the messages they hear that sex will make any relationship better, it's easy to start believing that, at the least, God is a bit old-fashioned. At the worst He is a cosmic killjoy.

Even some guys who believe in God try to make their own rules regarding sexual purity. They reason, "As long as I don't have sexual intercourse, it must be okay." These guys convince themselves that sexual contact with their hands and even oral sex are perfectly fine because they're not actually "having sex." They are wrong. They are connecting to girls in ways that God created exclusively for married people.

What these guys end up doing is creating a physical bond that leads to a chemical bond that ultimately results in an emotional bond with the girl. They don't realize that things are at work in their bodies at a deeper level than they realize. They don't understand the power of oxytocin and what it does to them.

# HOW YOU CAN BE DIFFERENT

This is a place where you have to choose
to believe and behave differently than most of the guys in our world. It will make you stand out as a bit strange, and it will never be easy.

Let's start with the belief part. You have to believe that God made sex to be something more than a biological drive. The fact that he put oxytocin in our bodies proves this. Believing this can give you a huge motivation to treat your sexuality as extremely precious. It can shift your thinking away from "I shouldn't have sex" and over to "I want to save sex for the one person that I will be connected to for life."

As you grow this belief into a strong conviction, your behavior will more easily get in line. While some guys you know are moving into sexual/physical contact with girls, you will be different. You will like girls and date girls, but you will focus on the relationship and their hearts, not their bodies. You will be able to truly get to know the girls you date without the confusion of a physical/emotional bond being created that isn't rooted in anything meaningful.

Know this: entering a boyfriend/girlfriend relationship where sexual contact isn't a key dimension is one of the most counter-cultural things you will do. It's just not normal in our world. But knowing what you know about oxytocin can motivate you to be different.

# FROM THE LIFE OF DAVID

Scripture tells us that David was a good-looking guy. His fame and position likely made him particularly attractive to women. You can be sure that he had no problem "getting the girl." In fact, the Bible mentions at least eight wives that he had (simultaneously) over his lifetime.

Again, we have a lot to learn from David. But when it

comes to women, we can learn mostly from what he did wrong.

Because he had children with most of his wives (there's a list in 2 Samuel 3:2-5), we clearly know that he had sex with them. Given what we know about how oxytocin works, this likely created a bond with each of these women that was hard to ignore. But it likely made for a bunch of "so-so" bonds as opposed to one powerful bond with one girl.

As God designed it, this intimate connection should happen between you and one woman for the rest of your life. If you are careless with who you are physically intimate with (like David), you run the risk of screwing up the good things that oxytocin can do in your marriage someday.

Here is one final thing to consider. Girls are generally more emotional than guys are. So, if oxytocin creates a powerful bond in the heart of a guy, we can be sure that it creates something even greater in a girl. Once a relationship turns physical, it can cause a girl to devote extreme amounts of energy and emotion to the relationship. It's one of the things that can make a girl obsess about a guy in ways that are very unhealthy.

This is the reason that breakups are so hard on girls. They have experienced a powerful bond with the guy that is difficult to break. Some studies show that our brains (fueled by oxytocin) become almost addicted to the other person. It's why you can see a girl continue to go back to a guy who everyone knows is no good for her.

The practical application for you is that you can't just connect with a girl emotionally and physically and then think it will end easily. Oxytocin complicates that. The more you connect, the harder it will be to end. When girls get physical (and then it ends) they can experience depression and sadness like many guys will never know. This chemical reaction truly has an emotional effect!

# TAKE ACTION

Beyond just a chemistry lesson about what happens when guys and girls connect physically and, you need some practical steps you can apply right now. Consider these things:

## 1. Believe that what you do now matters.

Most guys think that they can be a stupid teenager who can fool around with girls and then start being a responsible adult once they are older. They think that what they do now won't make a difference later. Your parents call this "sowing your wild oats." The logic is that if you get all your careless behavior out of your system when you are young, you won't struggle with it in adulthood. The reality of oxytocin proves that this is dead wrong. You need to believe differently.

## 2. Treat girls with tenderness.

On every date you go on and in every relationship you enter, remember this truth: girls are weaker than you. That's not just in terms of muscle mass and strength. That also applies to their hearts. They want to be loved and cherished and can thus be emotionally vulnerable to the attention of a young man like you.

Because of this, you must handle their hearts with great care, not giving too much of yourself to them (both physically and emotionally) until you are both ready. God designed that to happen in a covenant marriage. I'd wait until then.

## 3. Keep things in order.

A really smart guy named John Van Epp wrote a book called "How to Avoid Falling in Love With a Jerk." As the title clearly suggests, it's all about how to avoid ending up in a bad relationship. In it he describes what he calls the "Relationship Attachment Model." It includes five key dimensions of any romantic relationship, moving from "KNOW" all the way to "TOUCH."

# Relationship Attachment Model

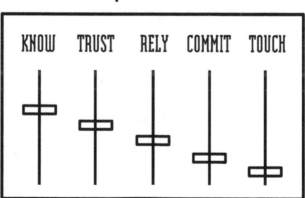

Van Epp's research suggests that healthy relationships move from left to right where first you know, then you trust, and move on through all five dimensions. Touch always comes last.

Couples frequently get this out of order and put the physical dimension of their relationship at the front end. These couples have a very high chance of being connected to the wrong person and eventually "falling in love" with a jerk. Remember, sex makes you stupid. Don't let this happen to you. Keep things in order. Keep your relationship from getting derailed by keeping the physical component out of the mix until much, much later.

Ultimately, you have to believe that your sexuality is precious and worth protecting. You can choose to exercise self-control now because you know it will pay off later. Consider this story told by South African pastor P.J. Smyth:

*When I lived in Harare, Zimbabwe, close to our apartment was the most enormous hole in the ground about the size of half a football field, and at least 40 feet deep. It was the foundation for a huge skyscraper office building. The bizarre thing was that during the pause in the work between digging the hole and starting to build, the site was totally unguarded for a few weeks. If I had the desire I could have got down into the bottom of the hole without much difficulty. Why were there no guards? Because there was nothing to protect, of course!*

*But let's imagine that for some reason I wanted to destroy the building. Rather than take a wrecking ball to it once it was up, I would be cunning to sneak down into the unguarded foundation, dig a couple of grave-size holes, lay some explosives that I set on a three year fuse, cover it over, climb out, walk away and relax for three years! And the beauty of it would be that they would probably never suspect that it was me!*

*In the same way, the foundation of your marriage is your pre-marriage years. If Satan can sneak in and mess you up during those foundational years, then he is well on the*

> *way to destroying your marriage in the future. The masterstroke of satanic genius is to make you believe that marriage only begins when you say, "I do."*

The research is clear (and God's Word is true): the more sexually active you are before marriage, the harder it is for you to have a meaningful sex life once you get married.

Whether you believe in the truth of God's Word or not, you can't deny the chemistry at work in our bodies. This stuff matters. The vast majority of your peers are unaware of the power of oxytocin and they don't handle it with care. Their relationships (and thus their hearts and lives) suffer, and they don't have a clue as to why it's happening.

Guys who want to be awesome (that's you) view their sexuality as something precious. You are motivated to guard it for the right reasons. It's not because God is some old-fashioned killjoy who wants to keep good stuff from you. No, it's just the opposite. You realize that He wants you to experience meaningful relationships and a great marriage someday.

Watch the video called Chapter 6 – Gnarls Barkley at www.infoforfamilies.com/awesome.

# TALK ABOUT IT

1. Have you ever witnessed or experienced a boy/girl relationship that seemed a bit dysfunctional, yet it kept on going? What part might oxytocin have played there?

2. Does understanding how oxytocin works give you a greater respect for God's command that we save sexual activity for marriage? Why or why not?

3. What practical responsibilities do you think God has given to guys who are in romantic relationships in regards to keeping things from getting too physical?

Vegetarian? That's a Latin word that means "bad hunter."

# 7. Becoming the Hero

*"With great power comes great responsibility."*
*- Stan Lee (Spider Man)*

Watch "Chapter 7 – Becoming the Hero" at www.infoforfamilies.com/awesome.]

If you watch any nature documentary about animals living on the plains of Africa, you're probably going to see a predator catching and eating another animal. It's what viewers want to see, and the filmmakers know it.

When you watch a lion moving in on several hundred antelope, the narrator (probably Morgan Freeman) points out the key to his strategy. In the midst of all those potential dinnertime choices, the lion identifies the weakest animal to chase. It might be old, young, or sickly, but he will always choose the most vulnerable animal to pursue. That's how a predator works.

Over the past year, I followed essentially the same thing in news reports coming out of California. But, the news wasn't reporting on lions and antelopes. In this case, the predator was a college guy and his prey was a drunk girl at a party. There's a lot to the story, but the short version is that he sexually assaulted her behind a dumpster while she was unconscious. It's sickening stuff.

According to the Centers for Disease Control – 1 in 4 girls are sexually assaulted before the age 18.

Why did he do it? We can't know for sure, but we know that the porn industry has trained young men to believe that girls always want sex. Perhaps in his mind, he was just doing what she wanted. Whatever the case, he gives us a worst-case scenario of what foolish young men are capable of.

Why did he pick her? Unfortunately, the young woman was very drunk. In her state, she couldn't adequately care for or protect herself. I'm not blaming her at all for what happened to her. But, like the weak and vulnerable antelope that the lion singles out, she was an easy target for a predator.

This particular incident made headlines because two guys on bikes caught the guy in the act and held him in place until the cops came. But stories like this happen all the time to high school students and on college campuses around our nation. Our sexually-charged culture has led some guys to believe that being aggressive like this is not a big deal.

Young men who are striving for awesomeness need to know that it's a big deal, indeed. Not only do you need to operate differently, but you need to be committed to protecting the weak around you from the predators that will always exist in our fallen world. It's how you become a modern day hero to those around you.

# THE BIG IDEA:

## Real men use their strength to guard and protect.

Chivalry is a concept that has been lost on your generation. First used as a word to describe the knights of medieval Europe, it was a code of ethics committed to courage under fire, protection of the weak, and honor for women.

A great example of chivalry can be seen in the men on the sinking Titanic. As the ship took on water, some declared "women and children first" when it came to filling the lifeboats. These men knew that they were likely declaring their own deaths in a few hours by giving their seats up for others.

What does it mean to be chivalrous in our world today? Different people might tell you different things, but there are a few key things that come to mind:

## 1. Chivalry Means Giving Honor

Every girl desires to be treasured and put upon a pedestal of honor. Ideally, this need will be met by a girl's father and she will expect nothing short of that from the other men in her life. Unfortunately, the fractured relationship between many fathers and daughters often causes girls to settle for far less than honor from men. While these girls may not demand honor and respect, you should give it nonetheless, because that is what chivalrous men do.

## 2. Chivalry Means Providing Protection

When a girl is with you (or even near you), you are taking responsibility for her protection and well-being. In extreme cases, this might require an extraordinary level of bravery and courage. One good rule of thumb is to guard and protect the girl exactly how her father would if he were right there with her. This takes maturity. You might have to learn to be aware of the dangers of your surroundings and circumstances like never before.

## 3. Chivalry Means Demonstrating Gentleness

Gentleness is not often a characteristic used to describe the typical teenager. And it implies far more than just having good manners. As you interact with the girls in your life, you can practice doing what God tells every husband to do with his wife: treat her as a "weaker vessel" (see 1 Peter 3:7). Relax, you don't have to "get in touch with your feminine side." In fact, it is just the opposite. True gentlemen are able to successfully channel their manhood in a way that is marked by both strength and tenderness; by an understanding that the feminine nature of women demands that you treat them differently.

> "Courtesy is as much a mark of a gentleman as courage."
> – Teddy Roosevelt

## 4. Chivalry Means Modeling Sacrifice

Chivalry means learning to love in a sacrificial way. Ephesians 5:25 commands husbands to be just like Christ in this way:

*"Husbands, love your wives, just as Christ loved the church and gave Himself up for her."* If this counter-intuitive calling toward selflessness is the expectation for Christian husbands, then you should practice doing it now, not later.

None of these things come easy. And none of them are particularly common among young guys today. But that's why being chivalrous enables you to stand out among the crowd. It's why it positions you to be an everyday (but significant) hero. It's also what will enable you, at the right time, to get the right girl.

The fact that we have to talk about this shows that our culture has come a long way. Back in the days of the Titanic, most men would naturally and instinctually give up their lives for women, even those they didn't know. Today, our women's liberation movement has programmed us to believe that there are no differences between the genders. This just isn't realistic. Men have been given a unique strength and we must use it.

## LISTEN TO YOUR BODY
# "WE ARE YOUR ARMS."

You know, the "gun show." From an early age, you probably flexed us to show off your strength. God gave you that strength for a reason: to guard and protect those who are weaker than you. So when you think of your arms, think of your need to always be prepared to help and care for others. This includes any and all women you encounter.

# HOW MOST GUYS OPERATE

My experience is that most young men tend to be users of women, not protectors. Many will grow out of it as they get older, but their teenage drives are particularly prone to self-centered behaviors and tendencies. Our culture has allowed it, and overly aggressive girls have permitted, even encouraged it.

It's not the girls' fault, but in many cases, their desire to be loved and wanted has caused them to lower their expectations of the men in their lives. In a nutshell, teen girls have allowed teen guys to get away with it.

Most teen guys don't spend a lot of time thinking about how to guard, protect, and care for the girls they encounter. They don't have evil intentions; they just don't know any better.

Some might have something of a "conquest mentality." This leads them to equate their manliness with how many girls they have been physical with. (These guys are idiots.) In the end, they might find themselves acting in stark contrast to the medieval knights who were first characterized by the word chivalry.

There will always be, however, a small percentage of guys who will deliberately take advantage of young women who have let their guard down. Sadly, the sexualization of our culture has forced many girls to choose between being "sexy" or being "invisible." Many girls choose poorly. Some might even let their guards down in an attempt to be noticed.

Given the opportunity, there will be a few guys out there who will attempt to exploit these girls sexually. They are the "worst of the worst," but they are out there.

# HOW YOU CAN BE DIFFERENT

The guys that you likely interact with in school, on the ball fields, and in the locker room are not your benchmark for how to treat women. Awesome young men like you have a higher standard. You are mindful of a "sixth sense" that enables you to tell that something isn't right about how the women around you are being treated.

Starting with your mother and your sisters, you can demonstrate some basic disciplines of chivalry. Put them first. Carry their loads, both physically and emotionally. Serve them well. Protect them from harm. As you begin to build these habits into your home life, it will be more and more natural to apply these behaviors and attitudes to all the women you encounter.

> Eating at restaurants like Hooters is the exact opposite of being chivalrous. You become a consumer of women, not a protector of them.

Because there will always be some guy looking for the opportunity to take advantage of a girl, you must always be on the lookout. Do all you can to protect the girls around you from that guy.

One more thing: If there is alcohol or drugs involved, you'll have to work extra hard. People typically make stupid choices when they are under the influence. So stay sober. And if push comes to shove, you may have to man up and actually push and/or shove the guy. That's just a part of being chivalrous.

DAVID

# FROM THE LIFE OF DAVID

If you are going to guard and protect women, you need to be on the lookout for red flags that scream "Someone needs help!" Again, we can look to David's family for an example of what to look for. In II Samuel 13:1-14 we read the tragic story of Amnon and Tamar, two of David's children from two different wives. It's a long story but well worth reading:

*In the course of time, Amnon son of David fell in love with Tamar, the beautiful sister of Absalom son of David. Amnon became so obsessed with his sister Tamar that he made himself ill. She was a virgin, and it seemed impossible for him to do anything to her.*

*Now Amnon had an adviser named Jonadab son of Shimeah, David's brother. Jonadab was a very shrewd man. He asked Amnon, "Why do you, the king's son, look so haggard morning after morning? Won't you tell me?"*

*Amnon said to him, "I'm in love with Tamar, my brother Absalom's sister."*

*"Go to bed and pretend to be ill," Jonadab said. "When your father comes to see you, say to him, 'I would like my sister Tamar to come and give me something to eat. Let her prepare the food in my sight so I may watch her and then eat it from her hand.'"*

*So Amnon lay down and pretended to be ill. When the king came to see him, Amnon said to him, "I would like my sister Tamar to come and make some special bread in my sight, so I may eat from her hand."*

*David sent word to Tamar at the palace: "Go to the house of your brother Amnon and prepare some food for him." So Tamar went to the house of her brother*

*Amnon, who was lying down. She took some dough, kneaded it, made the bread in his sight and baked it. Then she took the pan and served him the bread, but he refused to eat.*

*"Send everyone out of here," Amnon said. So everyone left him. Then Amnon said to Tamar, "Bring the food here into my bedroom so I may eat from your hand." And Tamar took the bread she had prepared and brought it to her brother Amnon in his bedroom. But when she took it to him to eat, he grabbed her and said, "Come to bed with me, my sister."*

*"No, my brother!" she said to him. "Don't force me! Such a thing should not be done in Israel! Don't do this wicked thing. What about me? Where could I get rid of my disgrace? And what about you? You would be like one of the wicked fools in Israel. Please speak to the king; he will not keep me from being married to you."*

*But he refused to listen to her, and since he was stronger than she, he raped her.*

Here you have two evil men who plot to take advantage of a girl. But all along the way you can see red flags of danger of where Amnon was obviously deceptive. He took steps to get the girl alone. He tricked her into getting physically close. Finally, he overpowered her, using his strength to prey on a girl who was weaker than himself.

In our fallen world, there will always be men like this. That's why God needs young men like you who will recognize the signs and then step in to protect the weak and vulnerable.

You might never need to physically protect someone from danger or harm, but you should be ready to do so. Beyond that, you can do a million little  things to demonstrate chivalry with the people in your life.

# TAKE ACTION

Start small, but start somewhere. You don't have to dress like a medieval night or anything weird like that. Consider these things:

## 1. Be a gentleman.

You can start by making the simple commitment to behave like a gentleman to the ladies in your life. And no, I'm not suggesting that you wear a top hat and invest in a cane. This isn't about what you wear. It's about how you speak to girls. (Do it with kindness and courtesy and with a commitment to encouragement.) It's about not being rude. (Watch your language, refrain from crass jokes, and put some controls on your burps and farts.)

## 2. Be on the lookout for warning signs.

You can always be in "guard and protect" mode with the other gender, especially when you're in a public setting with them. Guys usually aren't concerned about dark parking lots, but they make many women nervous. Be aware of things like that, and do whatever you can to make the girls around you feel secure.

Another thing: Tamar missed some of the warning signs that Amnon was trying to take advantage of her. Don't you miss them! To use a Spider Man reference, try to be attentive to your "Spidey sense." That's probably the Holy Spirit of God trying to tell you that something isn't right. You know what some guys are capable of, so don't allow some jerk to take advantage of a young woman on your watch.

### 3. In a relationship, protect the girl from you.

You might not realize it, but the guy in your mirror might be the one you have to most watch out for. When you first begin to dip your toes into a romantic relationship, becoming sexually intimate is a real possibility. Make sure to avoid situations that might lead to temptation for either you or the girl. Be aware of how easy it is to cross moral boundaries in your relationship and be committed to guarding the girl's reputation.

---

# How Far is Too Far?

Do you want a practical trick for knowing when you are crossing lines with a girl physically? God has given you a built-in barometer that tells you. (It's found in your shorts.) When that barometer begins to rise, you know it's time to stop doing whatever you're doing. Anything less than that is incredibly risky.

---

Let me tell just one more story about chivalry and then we will wrap this up. Several years ago, there was a Christian men's movement called Promise Keepers. Featuring big events in football stadiums, it encouraged men to be Godly and chivalrous. In a world that encourages us to treat men and women exactly the same, it caught some flak from a lot of folks on TV.

In the midst of all that, I saw an episode of "The View" where three of the four women panelists spoke harshly about the movement, insisting that it was a move backwards to a culture where wives had to follow the leadership of their husbands.

Then the fourth woman, who had been quietly listening to the debate up to this point, spoke up for the first time. I will never forget what she said. With firm conviction in her voice, this ardent feminist said, "You give me a man who will love and protect me like Jesus loves me, and I will follow him wherever he wants me to go." Well said.

What do you get when your life is marked by chivalry? When you make laying down your life to protect the women in your life a priority? When you learn to offer them sacrifice and selflessness? Eventually, you get the respect and commitment of the woman of your dreams. It may take a while to get there, but the payoff is so very worth it.

Believe this irrefutable truth: the guy with the six-pack abs might catch a girl's eye, but she will eventually grow weary of him. It will be the righteous and selfless young man of awesomeness who will get the girl in the end, even if he is a bit of a geek.

I know this from personal experience. So do many other men. Just look around at how many beautiful women you see married to average guys. I guarantee that they ended up together because the guys treated the girls in chivalrous ways that made them irresistible. Trust me on this. It matters.

Watch the video called "Chapter 7 – What Real Men Do" at www.infoforfamilies.com/awesome.

# TALK ABOUT IT

1. What does chivalry look like as you interact with your mom, sisters, and the other women in your daily life? (If you don't know, try asking them.)

2. Have you seen a "conquest mentality" among any of the guys you know? Do any of them talk about girls as targets to "score" with? How does that make you feel? What might you say in those situations?

3. When you begin to date, what are some practical ways to guard your romantic relationships from becoming physical?

Concealed weapons? You mean the hands in my pockets?

# 8. Finding Your Call Of Duty

*"Don't let anyone look down on you because you are young."*
*– I Timothy 4:12a*

Watch "Chapter 8 – Finding Your Call of Duty" at www.infoforfamilies.com/awesome.)

If you look back a few generations, you will find that a great deal has changed in what our culture expects of its young men. Just look at the men who have come before you to see how dramatic the differences are.

Your great-grandfather was probably from what many people call "The Greatest Generation." These are the guys who lived through the horrors of World War II and worked to rebuild America in its aftermath. Your great-grandfather probably knew some of the 18-22 year olds who bravely stormed the beaches of Normandy. All you have to do is watch *Saving Private Ryan* or *Band of Brothers* to see the huge responsibilities that were given to these young men.

Your grandfather probably came of age sometime during the 60's. As an 18 year old, he likely faced the real possibility of being drafted into the army. (That means he HAD to join up and go to war, even if he didn't want to.) The average age of the soldiers who fought (and died) during the Viet Nam war was 19. That means your grandfather's peers knew very well that graduating from high school meant adulthood. For those sent to war, it meant the possibility of death.

Things got a bit easier for your father's generation. While there were conflicts in the Middle East, he and his friends were never forced to go to war. Still, there was a sense that growing older meant growing up. For him (and me), there was an assumption that you would finish high school, get an education, and start a career. Moving back home with your parents was never an option.

Fast forward to today and your generation. Sociologist Michael Kimmel documented what you find in his groundbreaking book *Guyland*. After years of research, Kimmel determined that young men today have been allowed to remain boys for far too long. Where adolescence used to transition into adulthood by age 19 or 20, now (for many) adolescence lasts well past 25. An entire generation is wasting their lives with trivial things.

> "The only things that most 19-year old guys know how to do is play video games and masturbate." – Mark Driscoll

These young "men" might be educated and employed, but they are still functionally boys. Their lives are characterized by a desire to have fun and be entertained. Their money is spent not on the future or for a greater good, but on expensive toys and activities. They see girls as something to chase and use. They give no thought to growing up or having a life of purpose and meaning. At least not yet.

The third section of this "Guide to Awesomeness" is all about "how to save the world." After "guarding your heart" and "getting the girl," this is a third and essential part of building a great life. And while you might not literally save the world (you're not Jesus, and you're not a superhero), you are still invited by God to do something big with your life. It's a call that most of your peers will ignore.

# THE BIG IDEA:

## You can start now building a life that matters.

It's tempting to believe that your life doesn't matter, at least not yet. After all, you're probably still a teenager. But God wants you to know that He has big plans to use you for amazing things. And that doesn't have to start when you are "old." It begins now. The trajectory of your life is defined during these developmental seasons of life.

Even if your circle of influence is small, you can have a big impact. It all starts with taking a good look at your family, your friends, your school, your church, and anyplace else that God places you. Look for where God is at work and choose to join Him. The smallest acts of intention can truly have a lasting impact in the world. (Somebody had to tell a young Billy Graham about Jesus.)

> Evaluate your daily activities and your life's pursuits
> with this question: "Will this thing matter in 100 years?"

While you might not see big impact in the daily activities of your life, there are still things that are incredibly valuable during this developmental season you are in. Knowing that God is preparing you for big things can give purpose to what are often monotonous pursuits. For example:

# 1. Your Education

What you do in school can be a foundation for the opportunities you will have in the future. While this isn't always the case, having a solid education has the potential to open up greater possibilities for how God can use you. Remembering this might not help you with your algebra homework, but it can encourage you to attack it with purpose.

# 2. Your Character

Who you are is being formed during your teen years. Many of the choices you make and experiences you have will help define who you are becoming. Knowing that God is teaching you through both your wise and foolish choices can give purpose to the journey.

# 3. Your Relationships

Picking the right friends is critical during these years. Both the Bible and common sense tells us that we become who we interact with the most. That's why the friends you choose can help push you in the right direction. If your friends aren't thinking of anything beyond today, it is unlikely that you will give much attention to finding God's purpose for your life.

More than anything else, a young man trying to build an awesome life needs an eternal focus. You need to be consistently reminded that the things of this earth ultimately do not matter.

God gave you (and every other Christian) a clear purpose just before He went back to Heaven after the cross. In Matthew 28:19, He said, *"Go and make disciples."* The purpose of your life and the focus of your days should be somehow rooted in that calling. It can take a million different forms, but joining God in building His kingdom should be a part of it. That can happen whether you are 14, 40, or even 104 years old.

## LISTEN TO YOUR BODY
# "WE ARE YOUR LEGS."

The two of us make up the bottom half of your body, and we are here mainly for mobility, to move you from one place to another. Make sure your life is moving forward, not just standing still or simply going in circles. When you think of us, think of momentum. Even if you are young, your life can be moving in a clear and purposeful direction.

# HOW MOST GUYS OPERATE

Most of the guys you know are waiting until they grow up to do something meaningful with their lives. As described in the *Guyland* book, they are no longer boys but not yet men. They are *guys*. In their minds, they get to put off growing up for as long as they want.

Fun and entertainment are their main goals. Their lives are pretty boring so they are constantly looking for some way to distract their minds with something stimulating. Their phones are a constant companion because they always offer the false hope that something interesting will pop up there. Sadly, it's rarely satisfying. Like eating a bunch of candy, these guys are usually left longing for something more.

While their grandfathers fought real, blood and guts battles for important reasons, your peers are settling for video game battles. They are settling for a fake adventure because that's the best idea they can come up with. Unfortunately, no better narrative or plan has been offered to them.

# HOW YOU CAN BE DIFFERENT

As we said in the opening chapter of this book, you can be committed to telling a better story with your life. And, while you might not know today all that your story will include, you can commit to making it about something bigger than "entertain me."

Fully experiencing the "awesomeness" that God offers will require you to willingly step into some difficult things. It means finding something meaningful but seemingly impossible to tackle, the kind of thing that if God doesn't show up, you're going to fail. It means being scared but doing it anyway.

> "God has a way of picking a "nobody" and turning their world upside down, in order to create a "somebody" that will remove the obstacles they encountered out of the pathway for others."
> - Shannon L. Alder

Overcoming big challenges is what makes for a great story. If a video game is too easy, it becomes boring very quickly. The same is true for the life that you lead. You can choose to do the important but hard things that others won't do. It won't be easy, but it will certainly be interesting.

I'm not suggesting that you have to map out your entire life by age 15. What I am suggesting is that God's call for you to live a meaningful life starts now, not later.

# FROM THE LIFE OF DAVID

David was certainly not a guy who had a prolonged adolescence. From when he was young, his life was moving in a deliberate direction. In this area, there is much learn from him.

If you remember, David was anointed (clearly marked) as king of Israel while he was still a teenager. The prophet Samuel was led by God to go find the new king from among the sons of a man named Jesse. As all the strong and mature sons of Jesse were brought before the prophet one at a time, Samuel knew he hadn't yet found the right guy. We pick up the story in I Samuel 16:11-13:

*So he asked Jesse, "Are these all the sons you have?"*

*"There is still the youngest," Jesse answered. "He is tending the sheep."*

*Samuel said, "Send for him; we will not sit down until he arrives."*

*So he sent for him and had him brought in. He was glowing with health and had a fine appearance and handsome features.*

*Then the Lord said, "Rise and anoint him; this is the one."*

*So Samuel took the horn of oil and anointed him in the presence of his brothers, and from that day on the Spirit of the Lord came powerfully upon David.*

From that day forward, David's life had direction and purpose. While he wasn't yet the king, he knew that he had a big part to play in God's plan. This probably gave his thoughts purpose, even in the mundane parts of his adolescence. (Tending sheep probably wasn't the most exciting job in the world.) It also probably gave him confidence to serve in Saul's courts and to stand up to Goliath.

# TAKE ACTION

If you want to get your life moving in a more exciting direction, then you might have to start doing things a little bit differently than you are used to. Only God can show you what changes you need to make. But you can start with these simple things:

# 1. Look for the "time wasters" in your life.

You might be thinking that your life is too busy to consider the big issues of purpose and calling. Or you might think that you don't have time to do meaningful stuff with your life. While that might be true for some, the vast majority of us have plenty of free time. We just choose to fill it with frivolous things.

Identify some of the ways you spend your time that aren't helpful to your soul. Some common consumers of time include TV, video games, and just about anything else where a screen is involved. It may take some time to retrain your brain from its addiction to screens, but you can do it. Create a simple plan to cut back on something like 50% of the time you waste there. Then commit to doing something life-giving with the time you free up.

# 2. Start asking God the right question.

"What do you want to be when you grow up?" That's a question you have probably heard dozens of times throughout your life. I want to suggest that it's the wrong question. Even though it is well intentioned, it's rooted in self. It's all about what YOU want to be to give YOU a happy and satisfying life.

A better question to start asking God is this: "How do you want to use my life for your purposes?" This is rooted in God's plans for you. Throughout your teenage years and into adulthood, you can keep bringing your strengths, gifts, and experiences to God asking, "How can you use all that you have made me to be for big things in this world?" Slowly but surely, He will begin to show you.

## 3. Dream big dreams, but start where you are.

Believe that God has awesome and grand things in store for your life. Look towards your future with anticipation that He will use you to literally change the world. But don't get so focused on the distant future that you forget that He can use you in significant ways today.

All around you in big and small ways, God is constantly at work. He wants to use you to bring salt and light to a world that is bland and dark. He wants you to be His hands and His voice. Simply look for the people and circumstances where God's love and grace are needed. Then act. It's not complicated, but it requires you to pay attention and to move when God says move.

I think we can all agree that video games are awesome. But let's also agree that they are a poor substitute for a real life adventure. When you shut down your console, your heart is left empty. When you join God in creating a life of awesomeness, your heart is full. You have the satisfaction of doing something that actually matters.

Only Jesus can actually "save the world," but you can be a vital part of that in someone's life. And you will know that someone's life was changed because of your willingness to do what God calls you to do. So that's practically the same thing.

In the powerful war movie *Fury*, five American soldiers (and their tank) are called to stop the advance of a large group of German Special Forces. In a climactic scene, they must choose between running away or staying to fight, knowing that they will all likely die in the battle. In that moment, the outspoken Christian in the group quotes Isaiah 6:8:

*"Then I heard the voice of the Lord saying, 'Whom shall I send? And who will go for us?' And I said, 'Here am I. Send me!'"*

Needless to say, they all stayed to fight. This commitment to sacrificing their lives to save the lives of others is a perfect reflection of Christ's work on the cross. It is exactly what He did for you and me. And it is what He calls each of His followers to do, in turn.

Does that mean that you will have to die for Jesus? Probably not. But you must be willing to. In Mark 8:34-35, Jesus said, *"Whoever wants to be my disciple must deny themselves and take up their cross and follow me. For whoever wants to save their life will lose it, but whoever loses their life for me and for the gospel will save it."*

Get your life moving forward. Stop thinking about what the world offers and start dreaming about how you can give your life away for something that's bigger than yourself.

Watch the video called Chapter 8 – Christian's Story at www.infoforfamilies.com/awesome.

# TALK ABOUT IT

1. Do you think your peers are stuck in the extended adolescence described in "Guyland"? Why or why not? What do you see in them that makes you think that?

2. What are the things that you think will matter after you are dead and gone? What are some simple but purposeful things you can do today that actually might matter 100 years from now?

3. If there were no limitations and you were sure you would succeed, what big thing would you dream of doing for and with God?

Surrounded? You mean we
can attack in any direction?

# 9. Sharing Intimacy with God

*"The same God who created the universe with a word, now wants to speak to you." – Henry Blackaby*

Watch Chapter 9 - Sharing Intimacy with God at www.infoforfamilies.com/awesome.

Imagine going to your mailbox and finding a formal invitation addressed to you. Inside is information about a group of teenagers being formed to consult with a few key technology pioneers. Among them are Mark Zuckerberg (Facebook), Kevin Systrom (Instagram), and Tim Cook (Apple). You were randomly selected, and they want you to be in this group for the next decade, meeting with them four times a year in Seattle, San Francisco, Hawaii, and New York City.

Imagine researching it, making a few calls, and finding out that the invitation is totally legit. You have been given the chance to regularly interact with some of the people who are shaping the way our world connects. You would be developing a personal relationship with them, being invited into their world.

Imagine telling your friends about the opportunity. What if, after giving them the details, you told your friends that you had to turn it down? With everything you have going on, you just can't fit it into your schedule. You're just too busy.

If you told your friends that, how would they respond? My guess is that they would tell you that you are crazy. They would say, "Don't be an idiot! Drop everything to be a part of this. Rearrange your entire life if you have to. This is just too great of an opportunity to miss out on!"

While that would be an extraordinary invitation, I want you to consider an actual invitation that you have been given. No matter how long you have gone to church or been a Christian, I want you to take a fresh look at a mind-blowing reality. It's a truth that should blow your mind every time you consider it:

> The God of the universe has invited you to know Him personally.

Take a second and let that sink in. Seriously, think about it. The God who created everything and who knows everything has invited you to be close to Him. This should blow your mind. But for some reason it's likely that it doesn't.

It's like we have gotten this invitation in the mail from the Creator of everything and we respond by saying, "I can't do it. I'm just too busy. I can't fit God into my schedule right now." It's crazy.

God wants to give you an awesome life, but the foundation of that isn't what you do. It's Who you know. After all, you are not a human doing. You are a human being. And, first and foremost, you are called to BE in a love relationship with God. That's ultimately why you exist. It's why God created you.

I want you to know God's big plans for your life – His purpose for your days – it will always come out of your relationship with Him.

# THE BIG IDEA:

## You find God's will by staying close to Him.

This concept of being in a relationship with God is probably not new to you. You have probably been told that it's important to pray and talk to God. But I want you to consider exactly how relationships work: they are two-way. You probably know what it's like to talk to God. But how good are you at listening to Him?

> "My sheep listen to my voice; I know them, and they follow me."
> – Jesus in John 10:27

While God will speak to you most clearly through His Word, He also has given you His Holy Spirit. That's His very presence that is with you everywhere you go. And make no mistake, God has a voice. He wants to speak to you. He wants to tell you who you are and what to do.

You might not hear some loud booming voice coming to you from the clouds, but God's Spirit can quietly whisper to your heart and mind in ways that you know that it's Him talking. Does that sound strange? It shouldn't. That's what He consistently did in the Bible.

Think about all the people in the Bible who heard God's voice in some way: Adam, Noah, Abraham, Jacob, Joseph, Moses, Joshua, Gideon, Samuel, Elijah (and a bunch of other Old Testament Prophets), Peter, Paul, John, etc. The list goes on and on.

It was normal in the Bible for the people of God to hear the voice of God. Why would we think that when the Bible narrative ended that somehow God stopped talking to the people He loves and wants to lead? That makes no sense. In fact, it's ludicrous to consider a "relationship with God" without two-way communication.

> "Whatever is prominent in the Word of God should be conspicuous in our lives." – Charles Spurgeon

The key to staying close to God and hearing His voice is the simple act of being in love with Jesus. When you are in a love relationship with someone, you are motivated to be with them. The same holds true for God. You know how He has loved you and what He has done for you, so you respond with love. You want to know him, talk to him, and hear from him.

Unfortunately, so many of us follow God out of obligation or duty. Or maybe it's because our parents require it of us. It isn't a result of our devoted love for Him. If that's the case in your life, you are missing out on the essential reality of the Christian life.

## LISTEN TO YOUR BODY
# "I AM YOUR HEART."

While my functional purpose is to keep blood flowing in your body, I represent far more than that. The things you love have the power to drive your life, so make sure you are passionate about things that matter. Start with your relationship with God. Only when you stay intimately connected to Him can you discover a life of purpose.

"In Scripture we read of two kinds of men--the spiritual man controlled by the Holy Spirit, and the "carnal" man who is ruled by his passions." - David Jeremiah

# HOW MOST GUYS OPERATE

To be honest, most guys ignore God. Even if they believe in Him, they see Him as being far away and uninterested in their daily lives. They may even say that they are Christians, but their lives are certainly not connected to God. In II Timothy 3:2-5 these guys are described perfectly:

*"People will be lovers of themselves, lovers of money, boastful, proud, abusive, disobedient to their parents, ungrateful, unholy, without love, unforgiving, slanderous, without self-control, brutal, not lovers of the good, treacherous, rash, conceited, lovers of pleasure rather than lovers of God— having a form of godliness but denying its power."*

This harsh passage concludes by saying that these people have a form of Godliness, but that it's powerless. That's because they aren't truly connected to God through relationship. They keep God at a distance mainly because they don't want to submit to Him.

They have this picture of God being up in Heaven, sitting in the clouds and hanging out with a bunch of angels. He may be in charge, but He's distracted by other stuff. So these guys think they can do whatever they want and it's no big deal. They forget that God is always near them.

# HOW YOU CAN BE DIFFERENT

You can know that God is very, very close.
He is interested in every aspect of your life. You can have confidence that your most important relationship is with Him and that everything else in your life is dependent on being connected to Him. He has a voice and He wants to speak to you. He wants to lead you in the big and small things of life.

> "God is not just one thing we add to the mix called life.
> He wants an invitation from us to permeate everything
> and every part of us." – Francis Chan

In John 15:5, Jesus tells you about how important it is to stay connected to Him in relationship, *"I am the vine; you are the branches. If you remain in me and I in you, you will bear much fruit; apart from me you can do nothing."* That word "remain" implies staying consistently connected to Him, just like the branch of a vine. When you stay close to Him, good things happen. When you get disconnected, Jesus is very clear: you can do nothing of value. That's why it's so important to stay close.

If this all sounds familiar, it's probably because you have grown up in church and you have heard it all your life. The problem is that you can hear it so much that you stop hearing it. Or you start neglecting it. As a young man striving to be awesome, you can't afford to do that. You have to spend your days staying dependent on and hungry for God's presence in your life.

# FROM THE LIFE OF DAVID

While David was known for some significant screw-ups in his life, at his core was a man who desperately wanted to know God. This is what makes him such a great role model for us. He was flawed, but the foundation of his life was solid.

Listen to how God describes David in Acts 13:22, *"I have found David son of Jesse, a man after my own heart."* Something huge happens in the heart of a young man whose greatest desire is to know God and His ways. God takes both your strengths and weaknesses and uses it all for His purposes.

Throughout the Psalms (the songs that David wrote to and about God), you can see details of how he celebrated the bigness of God. But you can also see how he worked through his struggles. Sometimes it wasn't very pretty. He argued with God and even questioned God's faithfulness. He was honest.  But it's in the Bible, so we know his experience was okay.

One passage in Psalm 42:1-2 captures David's heart pretty accurately: *"As the deer pants for streams of water, so my soul pants for you, my God. My soul thirsts for God, for the living God. When can I go and meet with God?"*

David's desperate desire to know God was just as raw as a famished wild animal's desire for water. He wanted nothing more than to be in God's presence, to talk to Him and to hear His voice.

If you're honest, you would probably admit that you rarely feel that way about Jesus. Your heart is rarely that desperate. This is something that David got right that most young men do not. Perhaps it's because we're so distracted by everything else in our world.

David invites you into that experience with God when He challenges you in Psalm 34:8 to *"taste and see that the Lord is good."* The sad reality is that most Christian young men have never truly discovered how good and satisfying an intimate relationship with God can be.

What happens when you begin to walk daily with God? Like any meaningful relationship, He begins to impact your life. He changes you and makes you more like Himself. You start caring about the things that matter to Him. God starts leading you to do things that will make a difference in the lives of others. He gives your life (and your days) purpose and meaning.

Beyond all that stuff, the best thing you get when you walk with God is God. You get Him. Even if He doesn't call you to do awesome things (which He will), you get the incredible experience of knowing God. And again, that is the fundamental purpose of your life. Getting Him is enough.

# TAKE ACTION

There isn't some magical five-step process to walking with God. It's a relationship, and that requires love, commitment, and time. But here are a few good places to begin:

## 1. If you haven't already, start a relationship with God.

We can talk about *being* in a relationship with God, but you have to start by *entering* a relationship with God. It doesn't happen automatically. Because He is completely holy and you are completely sinful, you have to come to God on His terms. If you aren't clear on what that looks like, ask someone you trust. Or watch this short video. It will give you a good foundation of where to start.

Watch the video "Chapter 9 - Starting a Relationship with God" at www.infoforfamilies.com/awesome.

## 2. Cut out some of the noise.

It's hard to interact with a God you can't see when there are so many things fighting for your attention that you can see. You're probably a lot like those dogs in Pixar's movie *Up*. ("Squirrel!!") You're easily distracted. So you may need to de-clutter your life. Turn off the TV, turn off the music, and shut down your computer. And if what you are watching and listening to is garbage, you're clogging your spiritual mind with stuff that makes it even harder for God to speak clearly to you. Cut it out. Clean the junk out of your heart and mind!

## 3. Deal with any sin that is in the way.

In Matthew 5:8 Jesus said, *"Blessed are the pure in heart, for they will see God."* It's hard to hear from Him if your heart isn't pure; if there is habitual sin in your life. Let's be clear on something: if you have trusted Jesus with your life, you can be confident that your sins are forgiven. God isn't far from you. It's just that your sin has a tendency to make you run from God.

> Sin is plenty strong enough to create an ever-widening gap in one's relationship with God. The wider the gap, the less likely we are to pray. And the less we pray, the wider the gap becomes." – Bill Hybels

## 4. Start listening for His voice.

Find some times every day that you can be still, quiet, and connected with God. Talk to Him and be quiet long enough to let Him talk to you. And remember, God's voice will always match His Word. If you feel like God is telling you something that contradicts what you read in the Bible, you can be sure that's not Him. But if it aligns with the Word and character of God, then it's probably His voice that you're hearing. Have the attitude of young Samuel in the Bible: *"Speak Lord, your servant is listening."*

> Those people who know God's Word best
> usually hear God's voice the clearest.

God has a great plan for your life, but you will not be able to experience it until you are sharing intimacy with Him. That love relationship is what He wants most from you. When we are close to God, we are no longer motivated by guilt or obligation. We choose to do the right things because we want to please the One we love the most.

Maybe it's time to fully surrender your life to Jesus. Even if you remember trusting Christ at a young age, it might be time to "go all in" as a young man who has lived a little bit more. You know what rebellion and sin you are capable of, and you know that your corrupt heart needs rescuing. Perhaps it's time to enter a relationship with God like you have never experienced before.

If you are willing to admit it, you would probably say that the passion and longing that David felt for God is something you have never experienced. But it is possible. Because it's the most important thing in our lives, don't you think that God wants to help you to know Him intimately? You can make this your prayer:

*"God, I know you are real and I know you are the key to an awesome life, but I honestly don't love you like I should. I want*

*to have a passion for you and I want you to speak to me, but so many other things in this world distract me. Would you help me? Would you birth in me a desire for you like I have never known before? Help me to fall in love with you."*

He wants nothing more than to answer that prayer. He wants to draw close to you and show you how incredibly real He can be in your life.

Watch the video called "Chapter 9 - Michael's Story" at www.infoforfamilies.com/awesome.

# TALK ABOUT IT

1. Have you ever had a season of your life when you felt really close to God? What was it like? What did you do to foster the relationship?

2. Does it seem strange to think that God wants to speak to you? Why or why not?

3. What can you do right away that will enable you to connect with God in a more meaningful way? Deal with some sin? Cut out some noise? Start a relationship with Him for the first time? (Now don't just sit there. Do it!)

# 10. Staying on Track

*"When you stray from God's presence, He longs for you to come back. He throws His arms open, runs toward you and welcomes you home." – Charles Stanley*

Watch "Chapter 10 – Staying on Track" at www.infoforfamilies.com/awesome.

If you have gotten this far into the book and you're still keeping up, I want to say "atta boy" or give you a high-five or something. You're doing great. Hopefully you've learned something along the way. We're almost done, but I want to encourage you to hang in there just a little bit longer. This is perhaps the most important part.

Let's assume that you are committed to "guarding your heart." You know that sexual temptation is a real thing, and you are taking steps to avoid it.

You hope to "get the girl" one day, but for now you're striving to be the right kind of guy. You're trusting that God will grow in you a heart of chivalry and prepare you for the time when the right girl will come along.

Finally, you are open to how God will use you to "save the world," at least your part of it, anyway. You know that walking in intimacy with Him will give you the power and direction you need to make a difference in your sphere of influence.

If that's you (and I sincerely hope it is), then you are well on your way to awesomeness. That's the good news. But there's a little bad news, as well. It has to do with God's enemy and his big objective in your life.

When you are focused only on your self-centered life, you are not much of a concern to Satan. He knows that he has deceived you sufficiently that your life is focused mainly on the things of this earth. At that point, he leaves you to your own bad habits and patterns, showing up only when he wants to get your life even more screwed up. But for the most part, you are not his concern.

But the minute you commit to something meaningful in your relationship with God, it's like putting a target on your back. Satan knows that you will be available to God for His purposes, and Satan hates that. He wants nothing more than to get you off track.

So he will tempt you. He will distract you. He will try to convince you that the things that will give you life will actually make you miserable. Just like in the Garden of Eden, he will lie to you about God's intentions. Even though he is a defeated enemy, he still has influence. Even though God's power will always overcome him, Satan will still try to derail your life from the things that matter.

While you know better and will strive to believe God's truth over Satan's lies, it's very likely that a time will come when you will stumble. You will sin. Even though David had a passionate heart for God, he still fell. But what's important is what happens after you fall. This chapter is all about what you should do when you blow it. Because you WILL blow it.

# THE BIG IDEA:

## Dealing openly with your sin is the key to overcoming it.

When you sin, the last thing you want to do is to deal with it openly. If you are like most people, your tendency is to go dark; to hide. You experience some measure of shame, so you want to push it down as deep as possible. You think, *"Whatever I do, don't let anyone find out. Especially God."*

This is exactly what Adam did in the Garden of Eden. He knew he had disobeyed God so he hid. He didn't want God to know about it. As illogical as that sounds, we tend to do the exact same thing. We convince ourselves that we can keep on going about our business and that God will never find out.

> "Hiding your sins from God."
> Have you ever heard of anything quite so ridiculous?

In the meantime, the sin grows like a cancer in our hearts and souls. But it doesn't have to be that way. While we are hiding out, God is saying to us, *"I'm God. I know your every thought and deed. I saw what you did. It's not good, but I still love you. So stop hiding. Come to me, confess the sin, and experience the grace that I poured out to you on the cross. Let's deal with it and get back to sharing our love relationship. We don't have time to waste on you running away from me."*

When we get stuck in habitual sin, running from God is what we tend to do. The shame and guilt of the whole thing leads us to convince ourselves that God has lost patience with us. That He is mad at us. So we avoid Him. We tend to forget that He is the solution to all of our problems. We forget that He loves us even when we blow it.

## LISTEN TO YOUR BODY
# "WE ARE YOUR KNEES."

We will be critical to your journey in life. When you blow it and let God down, don't run and hide. Instead, think of us. Humbling yourself before God and confessing your sin is the first and best place to start. He knows what you did and He loves you anyway. So don't use your feet and run; use your knees and pray. Get right with Him before you do anything else.

# HOW MOST GUYS OPERATE

While some people might try to hide their sins, many guys outright deny that they even exist. They will convince themselves that their particular disobedience to God's truth is no big deal. After all, everybody does it. So what's the problem?

Even if they do acknowledge their sin, they might try to justify it through comparison. They will pick the most famous and notorious evildoers on the planet to compare themselves to. *"At least I didn't murder anyone. Compared to Hitler, I'm a saint!"* The problem is that we don't get to compare ourselves to others. We have to compare ourselves to God.

# HOW YOU CAN BE DIFFERENT

To be awesome, you need to stay in a right relationship with a holy God. That means recognizing that even in your "smallest" of sins, you fall way short of His holiness (See Romans 3:23). But because of His extravagant love, you can accept the grace He offers and be immediately restored to Him. But this starts by dealing honestly and openly with your sin.

The operative word here is confession. When God convicts you or someone close to you confronts you about a sin, the best thing you can do is admit it. When you bring it into the light, it loses its power over your life. You can agree with God that it was foolish, receive the forgiveness He generously offers, and then move on.

That's exactly how God operates. But somehow, we have believed the lie that it is much more complicated than that.

# FROM THE LIFE OF DAVID

There is a textbook example of sin, confession, and restoration from David's life. Do what he did and you'll be headed in the right direction to staying right with God.

David had sex with a woman who wasn't his wife and then had her husband murdered. I think you would agree that his sins were pretty significant. God responded by having his prophet Nathan confront David directly, calling him into account for the things he had done.

David's response is so important. He didn't deny, downplay, or make excuses for his behavior. You can read exactly what he said in 2 Sam 12:13:

> "Then David said to Nathan, 'I have sinned against the Lord.'
> Nathan replied, 'The Lord has taken away your sin. You are not going to die.'

David owned it. He compared what he had done with the character and calling of a holy God and he confessed that he had fallen well short. And he was forgiven. No shame. No guilt. No grudge held by God against Him. He was made right by a God who forgives.

Note that this wasn't an insincere admission of guilt just to get out of the consequences. There were still plenty of those. But you can see just how truly broken he was when you read his full confession.

Take a minute to open your Bible and read David's confession in Psalm 51. It's pretty long but it's a good read. Think about how your typical confession of sin is like or unlike David's.

Once we confess, we need to follow up with the right response. To maintain our purity and to stay on track, we need to make sure we are hard in the right places and soft in the right places. Let me explain what I mean.

When dealing with things like sexual sin, we need to go hard on external boundaries and go easy on internal things like our identity. For example, to overcome sexual temptation, you might need some hard, firm boundaries in your life regarding your technology. You might need to do something radical like tossing your phone or ending a relationship. But you need a soft response when it comes to your identity. You need to be reminded that you are loved. You are good. You are forgiven.

Unfortunately, most people get this reversed. They go soft on external boundaries and hard on internal things like identity. They don't put any real accountability in place to keep them from sin. But they are extremely hard on themselves when it comes to the status of their hearts. They believe that they are bad people who deserve condemnation and punishment. They believe Satan's lies that say, *"God doesn't want to have anything to do with you. So don't bother going to Him."*

That's not the gospel. God is always willing to forgive. His grace is extravagant. Like the father to the prodigal son, He waits and watches for us to return to Him. When we do, He runs to welcome us home. He lovingly greets us with open arms. That's the nature of our Father.

# TAKE ACTION

When you know that you have sinned, there are four simple steps that you should walk through with God:

## 1. Admit that you blew it.

Before seeking God's forgiveness, you must first recognize that what you have done is sin. If you are going to move towards getting right with God and others, you must first be willing to admit that you have fallen short of God's ideal. Hopefully, you will feel a burden of responsibility and recognize the need to make it right.

## 2. Turn from your sin and accept God's complete forgiveness.

Once you acknowledge your sin, the next element of redemption is critical. Sadly, it is the part that you probably tend to get wrong. Because of Jesus, you don't get punishment and guilt for your sin. Instead, you get grace and forgiveness. Your slate is wiped clean. God deals with you not on the basis of your sin but on the basis of what He did for you at the cross.

## 3. Make changes to avoid the same mistakes in the future.

If you make a commitment to "go and sin no more" but do not take steps to adjust your life, you probably won't see much long-term change. Practically speaking, that means you might need to remove some obvious temptations from your life.

In addition to cleaning out some of the obvious stumbling blocks in your life, you will want to replace them with a renewed commitment to walking with Christ, feeding on the Scripture, and living in Christian community.

# 4. Live in freedom.

Just as the forgiving work of Christ on the cross is the solution to the sin of your past, it is also what you can look to for hope for the future. Your rebellious heart leads you to believe that turning from sin and pursuing righteousness is an impossible pursuit. The enemy will try to convince you that it's too hard: *"You can never measure up to God's standard, so don't even try."*

You must remember that Jesus came to set the captives free. Picture the powerful breakout scene from *The Shawshank Redemption*. After more than twenty years of suffering in chains, Andy Dufresne is finally free. His outstretched arms and jubilant expression tell the story of what he feels inside. In contrast to his previous bondage, he now tastes the joys of freedom.

Paul writes in Galatians 5:1, *"It is for freedom that Christ has set us free. Stand firm, then, and do not let yourselves be burdened again by a yoke of slavery."* With complete and unconditional forgiveness comes full and complete freedom. Satan doesn't want you to believe that, but it's still true.

Some days, it can be a challenge to see your new life in Christ as the source of ultimate freedom. That's why you have to realize that complete and lasting joy can only be found in full surrender of your life to Jesus.

When I was a teenager, I had a lousy understanding of Christ's core message. My Christian life was motivated by fear and guilt, not freedom. This belief ultimately pushed me away from Christ, as I felt I could never bring my game up to the level of His expectations. If I couldn't measure up (and thus felt distant from Him), then I needed to work hard to get my act together before I came to Him.

In some ways I felt like God was pleased with some future version of me, not the person that I was in the here and now. I loved God and wanted to please Him, but I spent many years running from Him simply because I didn't understand the simple wonder and beauty of the gospel: *"Come as you are. God will make you right."*

Let's all agree that it is incredibly difficult to bring your sinful nature into submission. You might fight some temptations all your life. But it is entirely possible to walk in victory. It just requires a commitment to "crucify the flesh" that is constantly at war with your soul.

Crucifixion was used by The Roman Empire as their primary means of execution. We know what they did to Jesus, but He was one of tens of thousands of people who they nailed to crosses. It is in that context that Paul wrote in Galatians 5:24, *"Those who belong to Christ Jesus have crucified the flesh with its passions and desires."*

Every Roman soldier knew that when you drive nails into someone, he resists. But eventually, he will tire and submit. Do it long enough, and they will stop fighting altogether. You are called to do the same thing to your flesh: to crucify it.

While it might feel like you will never overcome your sinful nature, it will eventually submit if you keep on crucifying it. This is true even if you have damaged your brain with years of bad habits. After all, God is still in the business of transforming every part of your life. He has the power to reset your mind.

This is critical to staying on track. Even though the enemy has placed a great big bull's eye on your back, you can walk in victory. Even when you blow it, you can run to the God who offers forgiveness and grace. And our God will continue to lead and guide you towards His very best for your life.

Watch the video called "Chapter 10 – Forgiveness" at www.infoforfamilies.com/awesome. It's a graphical collection of quotes about forgiveness from the teaching of Matt Chandler. It's truly life-changing stuff.

# TALK ABOUT IT

1. When you commit a private sin that nobody knows about, do you tend to "run and hide" from God? Why or why not? How's that working for you?

2. Is it easy to believe that God loves some future, better version of you, but not the current you? Why is it so hard to believe that God loves you completely just as you are?

3. What can you do to "crucify the flesh" in your life? Are you encouraged to know that your sin nature will eventually submit and stop fighting against you? Do you believe that?

Deadly flu going around? Good, my immune system is getting rusty.

# 11. Feeling the "Heaviness" of These Things

*"The night is darkest just before the dawn.*
*And I promise you, the dawn is coming."*
*- Harvey Dent in The Dark Knight*

Watch "Chapter 11 – Feeling the Heaviness of These Things" at www.infoforfamilies.com/awesome.

Our world is broken. Almost seven billion people share this planet and they all have their own ideas of what Truth is. Most of them are wrong and end up leading lives of hopelessness. Through Jesus, God has offered humanity purpose and an invitation to a relationship with Himself. But sadly, most people ignore Him.

In the midst of the darkness, you can't afford to lose hope. For just as the disciples thought all was lost when Christ died on the cross, Sunday morning brought a whole new reality. Jesus was alive and well. He showed us that if He can overcome death, He can overcome anything.

Jesus in the process of restoring the world. It's not going to fully happen until He returns someday, but He is using His people during these last days to build His kingdom here on earth. And he invites you to be a part of it.

You may think, "I'm just a kid." This is true, but it doesn't matter. God loves using young people like you for big things. David kills Goliath as a teenager. Jeremiah is called to be a prophet as a teenager. Mary gives birth to Jesus as a teenager. God can and will use you no matter how young or old you might be.

These days are critical. As we have already said, in many ways, the trajectory of your life (particularly in character and values) gets set when you are young. You just can't afford to wait until you "grow up" to start thinking about your place in God's plan.

This dark world needs God's light, and you are just the person to bring it. With such a huge shortage of strong, passionate, Godly young men in our world, there is a need for guys like you to stand up and be counted. To be awesome.

# THE BIG IDEA:

## The world is counting on you.

You need to note that the big idea is not that "God is counting on you." That would suggest that He needs you. He doesn't need anybody. He's going to have his way whether you step up or not.

But he invites you to join Him in saving the world, to take part in His plan to draw all people to Himself. And that's absolutely thrilling. It's something I definitely want to be a part of. You do, too. Especially in the lives of people you know. Even more so in the lives of the people you haven't met yet. There are a ton of people that you do not know but that you will one day have an incredible love for.

I'm talking about your descendants, your children and grand-children and all the generations that will follow behind you. When you think about it, that's (potentially) a whole lot of people.

I did the math on this once. I have five kids. Imagine if each of my kids gets married and has five kids and each of my grandchildren get married and have five kids. Imagine that goes on and on for generations. Do you know you many descendants I will have in just 8 generations? When you count all the sons-in-law and daughters-in-law, it's something like 950,000 people. Seriously.

> Steve Farrar puts it this way: "I may not know my great-great grandchildren. But my great-great grandchildren will know me."

You're going to leave a legacy to a bunch of people that you might never meet. That's why what you do today truly will echo in eternity. That's why you can't afford to mess around with your life; especially when it comes to your sexuality.

This book started off with the suggestion that one particular part of your anatomy has a great deal of influence over your life. Poor sexual decisions can derail your future. They can also cause immeasurable damage to the tender hearts and lives of any girls that you are careless with.

Watching "Shark Week" one night, I learned that you can tell that a Great White shark is female by it's scars. Apparently, mating for Great Whites is aggressive and the females usually end up wounded in the process. What's true in the animal kingdom is true for us, as well: "(premarital) sex means scars."

For many Christian men of conviction, their greatest regrets in life are the emotional and spiritual scars they left on the girls they dated in high school and young adulthood. God is able to heal and to give us a fresh start, but the wounds you experience and the wounds that you inadvertently cause in others are not easily resolved. They become that baggage that you (and others) will take into your marriage and your future. You have to take this seriously.

## LISTEN TO YOUR BODY
# "WE ARE YOUR SHOULDERS."

There is a classic phrase that features us: "There's a lot riding on your shoulders." It means that you have a big responsibility and that what you do (or don't do) matters. What you do with your life will have a big impact on the world and how it sees God. There are lives you will impact through every one of your good and bad decisions. You should walk through life aware of the heaviness of this reality.

# FROM THE LIFE OF DAVID

There are powerful moments in the movies when you see a father giving his son a final word before he dies. We call this a "deathbed speech." It's usually something incredibly meaningful that rights a lifetime of wrongs and affects the course of the young man's life.

In I Kings 2:1-3 scripture records the final words that David gave to his son Solomon before he died. And like in the movies, we have the opportunity to listen in on the important things that our hero shares before he breathes his last breath.

*"When the time drew near for David to die, he gave a charge to Solomon his son. 'I am about to go the way of all the earth. So be strong, act like a man, and observe what the LORD your God requires: Walk in obedience to him, and keep his decrees and commands, his laws and regulations, as written in the Law of Moses. Do this so that you may prosper in all you do and wherever you go.'"*

David wants his son to prosper. He reminds Solomon that there are few non-negotiable keys to making that happen: walking with God, obeying His commands, and trusting that His ways are best. If you shortcut these things, you will miss out on the awesome life God has in store for you.

# TAKE ACTION

As you live out a life of awesomeness, there are a few final things to incorporate into your days. And these aren't just one-time actions steps, but things you should value throughout your life. Start doing these things now, but keep doing them in some way until the day you die:

## 1. Have a band of brothers.

David had a best friend in Jonathan. The two of them were incredibly tight. David also had an army of faithful men that literally had his back during some very difficult days. Deep, meaningful relationships like this will be invaluable to you.

You need more than just good friends. You need other men who understand the life you are trying to build and who will push you towards it. They understand because they are striving to build that kind of life as well. These friends will celebrate great times with you, but they will be the ones who will be at your side when times are hard. They will also confront you when you are doing something stupid.

The friendships that guys have can tend to be shallow, so you'll have to make some effort to go deep. Two activities foster this: doing something difficult together and openly sharing your struggles with one another. Men used to find "difficult" in the foxholes of war, but you can find it on a mission trip or in raising your families in close proximity.

For the "sharing your struggles" part, ask God to lead you to a friend who you can start being painfully honest with. As you share your struggles in standing strong with God, it's likely he will do the same. You'll be surprised how God will use you to be "iron sharpens iron" friends. Once you have this kind of relationship, be loyal until the day you die.

## 2. Look for men you want to be like and ask them for help.

Our world has become so isolated that we have missed out on the "relational discipleship" that Jesus modeled perfectly with his disciples. Jesus knew what we have forgotten: the best way to grow and change is by hanging out with people you want to be like, inviting them in to your life and world.

So all along your journey through the stages of manhood, look for men who you want to be like, men who are building lives of awesomeness. Ideally, they will be about one life-stage ahead of you. Watch what they do. Ask them questions. Learn from them. Beg them to show you the way. Your father might be a great person to start watching, but find other men as well. You probably learn best when you have an example to follow, so find one.

As you build relationships with those who are ahead of you, don't forget to look behind you. Even if you don't feel capable or "arrived," there will always be someone younger than you who needs you to invest in him. Even if you don't feel like you have much to give, an amazing thing happens when you mentor someone else. It forces you to grow and to depend upon God. You both mature in the process, and that's a very good thing.

# 3. Tell a God-sized story with your life.

The first two steps were about your relationships with other guys, but this one goes back to your relationship with God. As you walk with Him and see how big and how active He is in the world, you can commit to finding a big part in the story He is telling.

Begin now to ask Him for big dreams of a life of impact. Make sure your dreams are rooted in His Kingdom, and then make them huge. Never stop dreaming about what God might do in you and through you. The Bible is full of stories of God doing enormous things through regular people just like you. He's still telling His story. Be the type of man who people will write about someday.

As young men of awesomeness walk with God and keep His commands and live in light of eternity, great things will happen. Men like this (and like you) will lead rich, meaningful lives of purpose and the world will be changed.

At some point, each man who has submitted His life fully to Jesus will stand before God. At some point, YOU will stand before God. You will give an account for how you managed the life He gave you. Jesus illustrates it this way in Matthew 25:14-21:

*"It will be like a man going on a journey, who called his servants and entrusted his wealth to them. To one he gave five bags of gold, to another two bags, and to another one bag, each according to his ability. Then he went on his journey. The man who had received five bags of gold went at once and put his money to work and gained five bags more. So also, the one with two bags of gold gained two more. But the man who had received one bag went off, dug a hole in the ground and hid his master's money. After a long time the master of those servants returned and settled accounts with them. The man who had received five bags of gold brought the other five. 'Master,' he said, 'you entrusted me with five bags of gold. See, I have gained five more.' His master replied, 'Well done, good and faithful servant! You have been faithful with a few things; I will put you in charge of many things. Come and share your master's happiness!'"*

---

You want to hear God to say, "Well done!"

---

You want to be a good steward of the life He has entrusted to you. Don't take what God has given you—whatever that might be—and bury it in a hole. Nurture it. Grow it. Use it. Share it. Build it.

As God leads you, make every day you live meaningful. Do the hard work of guarding your heart. When the time is right, invite a girl to join you in your adventure. As you strive to make each day awesome, you'll discover down the road that you're actually living an awesome life. It is in God's heart that you experience exactly that.

So get going. . .

# TALK ABOUT IT

1. Have you ever considered the impact your life today might have on your great-great grandchildren? What do you want them to look back and think of you?

2. Who are the "band of brothers" friends that God has given you during this season of life? What can you do to take things deeper in your relationship?

3. Who are some older men that you can start striving to be more like? What steps can you take to invite yourself into their life?

If you are a parent and want to explore these issues a little bit deeper, you'll want to get "The Talks." It covers everything you need to help your kids navigate our hyper-sexualized culture.

# —THE— TALKS

A parent's guide to critical conversations about sex, dating and other unmentionables.

www.INFOforFamilies.com

CPSIA information can be obtained
at www.ICGtesting.com
Printed in the USA
LVHW03s0833031018
592132LV00003B/25/P

9 781541 160095